PRAISE FOR THE AUTH
CHANGE IS THE RULE: PRACTICAL
ON TARGET, ON TIME AND ON BUDGET &
RED ZONE MANAGEMENT:
CHANGING THE RULES FOR PIVOTAL TIMES

Double Day Select Executive Program Book Club Alternate Selection

"You don't have to be afraid of change any longer! Change is the Rule offers entertaining and simple solutions that will help you move swiftly and efficiently through the growing pains of organizational change."

Ken Blanchard
Co-author, The One Minute Manager and Leadership by the Book

"Just brilliant!" In his book "Change is the Rule" Dr. Winford E. 'Dutch' Holland expands on the metaphor of the organization as a theatre company - and it is brilliant! It's brilliant because it simplifies understanding - it reduces the complexities of organization change to common sense with a very clear 'picture' to relate to. It is a very powerful metaphor that is very easily understood and 'got' by almost anyone who has ever been to any type of theatre presentation.

Rick Sidorowicz From *Best of The CEO Refresher on Leading Change*

"What a great uncluttered roadmap for understanding, embracing, and leading change. We have trained over 10 million leaders worldwide, and change is their biggest challenge. This book should be next on their reading list!"

Dr. Paul Hersey, Chairman
Center for Leadership Studies
"Home of Situational Leadership"

"Organization change - on target, on time and on budget... what a concept! How easy it is to forget these fundamentals when we leap off the cliff of organizational change! The basics aren't new - but they're organized in a way that you want to slap yourself on the forehead and say "why didn't I think of that"!"

Katherine M. Tamer
Vice President and Chief Information Officer
United Space Alliance

...a Red Zone loss could mean irrecoverable losses for your company. Among conditions that flag a Red Zone: major shifts in competitive strategy, mergers, culture changes, and implementation of new computer systems. Principles for success under Red Zone conditions include practical advice such as, "Put the Best Players in the Game." Holland points out that "if you select your organization's best for the Red Zone and your key executives are not on that list,...you may want to do some re-staffing." **Red Zone Management** pulls few punches, and its perspective is likely missing from many a boardroom.

Harvard Business School
Working Knowledge

These days we are constantly inundated with new books on the topic of management. However, <u>Red Zone Management</u> rises above the rest. It should be required reading for all managers, both to familiarize junior managers with the red zone management concept as well as to fine tune the inherent red zone management skills of senior managers.

Mark A. Wallace,
President & CEO,
Texas Children's Hospital

Multiple rapid changes, successfully executed, will be the key to the 21st century business. 'Dutch' lays it out—change must be managed. To expect transformation without good management is a dream. This is a book that must be 'on the desk' of a successful 21st century CEO.

Major General John S. Parker, M.D., Commanding General
USA Medical Research and Material Command
Fort Detrick, Md

"**Red Zone Management** is a new, creative and comprehensive treatment of a complex and seldom understood subject. I could not put the book down until I had finished reading it. The book is packed with case histories of business success and failures with comments for why the outcome was as it was. In the past while being involved in a major merger, my company successfully utilized the principles described by Dutch. The results were that the whole was greater than the sum of the parts--a resounding success for the shareholders.

M. P. Corky Frank, President
Marathon-Ashland Petroleum

IMPLEMENTING TELEMEDICINE

COMPLETING PROJECTS
ON TARGET ON TIME ON BUDGET

Robert Cuyler, PhD and
Dutch Holland, PhD

To order additional copies of this book, contact:
Xlibris Corporation
1-888-795-4274
www.Xlibris.com
Orders@Xlibris.com
111778

Dedication by Robert Cuyler

My deep appreciation goes to my wife Sally Davis and my children Zachary and Natalie who have encouraged and supported me in the balance of work and family. My thanks also to my business partner and mentor Jack Behnke who greatly helped this 'bookish' psychologist make the transition from practitioner to entrepreneur and business leader.

Dedication by Dutch Holland

This book is dedicated to the kids in my life: the little kids, Hope, Win, and Everett (E.J.) as well as the big kids, Eric Wendy. May they continue to flourish – and God Bless!

TABLE OF CONTENTS

Preface .... **xi**

The Promise and State of Telemedicine
- The Good News and the Bad News about Telemedicine
- The Implementation of Telemedicine in Healthcare Organizations
- The People Variables Have a Major Impact on Implementation
- The Technology Variables Have a Major Impact on Implementation
- Critical Success/Failure Factors in Telemedicine Projects
- The Purpose of this Book

Foreword .... **xxv**

Successful Organizational Change
- The management imperative to lead change
- Understanding organization change as a transition project
- Understanding organizations as a collection of "moving parts"
- Identifying the change projects that will drive the organizational change
- Identifying the change projects within the change projects
- This book and how it might be used

Chapter One **1**

Introduction to Organizational Change Management
- The leader's job is to guide organizational change
- The universal metaphor for understanding organizational change
- Understanding Change Projects as "Changing the Play"
- Using the theatre metaphor to understand the formula for change
- You know where you are

Chapter Two **25**

Communicate a Clear Vision for Telemedicine
- Construct the Detailed Vision for transition to Telemedicine
- Construct the Case for Change to Telemedicine
- Ensure Management Understanding and Expectation
- Communicate the Vision the Right Way to the entire organization
- Ensure Employee Translation of the Telemedicine Vision

Chapter Three **51**

Alter Work Processes and Procedures for Telemedicine
- Identify Process Alterations Needed for transition to Telemedicine
- Alter and Test Processes Critical for a Transition
- Alter Process Measures, Goals, and Objectives to Fit the Vision
- Alter and Test Work Procedures for Altered Processes
- Eliminate Old Measures, Goals, Objectives and Procedures

Chapter Four **71**
Alter Facilities, Equipment, and Technology (FET)
- Identify the FET alterations needed for transition to Telemedicine
- Alter and test all the FET needed in each transition
- Alter and test each and every FET control
- Alter or create written guidelines for all involved FET
- Eliminate old FET and operating guidelines

Chapter Five **99**
Alter Performance Management
- Identify / Alter Individual Roles / Goals Needed for transition to Telemedicine
- Complete One-on-one Contracting for Every Person affected by the Transition to Telemedicine
- Train All Employees in the Roles they will play in Telemedicine
- Identify and Alter the System for Monitoring Performance
- Alter and Communicate Compensation Payoffs for New work

Chapter Six **139**
Manage Change as a Project
- Set and Communicate the Master Schedule for transition to Telemedicine
- Use Week-at-a-time Transition or Implementation Scheduling
- Make One-on-one Transition Assignments
- Regularly Measure Transition Progress and Reschedule
- Confirm and Celebrate the Completed Transition

Chapter Seven **179**
And in Conclusion ...
- The Management Imperative to Lead transition to Telemedicine
- The Requirement to Successfully lead Transition Projects
- The message to Healthcare Managers

Appendix A **185**
Task List for Successful Organizational Change

Appendix of Detailed Steps and Scripts for Selected Chapters... 187

A NOTE TO THE READER

> *Each of us wants content "served up" in the way that best works for us. Deep down many of us wish "to get the answers in a few clever and memorable sound bites ("If the glove don't fit, then you must acquit...!" or "If they just don't get it, keep yelling until they regret it!") Sorry, but the explanation of the weighty and important concepts of successful organizational change takes more than sound bites. We have, however, written the book to be as accommodating as possible with three options for gaining value from our content. Good luck!*

Option One: I just want the "meat," please!

If you are looking for a proven, easy-to-understand, easy-to-use model for successful organizational change, this is the right book. Just read the Foreword to get the idea that successful organizational change is all about breaking change into projects and then completing those projects ... on target on time, and on budget. Then read Chapter One to get the key idea that changing an organization is like a theatre company stopping an old play and transitioning to a new one ... on target, on time, and on budget. And that's the meat? Yep, that's all there is to it ... except for a few million details we will cover in the following chapters. (Not really, we will only cover a couple of dozen important action steps.)

Option Two: I just want to know about the people-side of change, please!

That seems to be a reasonable request and we will try to help you out, although we will do so with some reluctance. As you read in Option One above, you should read the Foreword to get the "change projects ideas," Read Chapter One to get the "theater company transitioning to a new play idea," if after reading those two chapters, you still want to restrict your learning to the people side of change, if you just want to know how to transition actors to a new play without worrying about all the trivial and irrelevant stuff like the script, the roles, the sets, props, and the contracts (since none of the aforementioned items need not in any way affect the actors in a play or workers in an organization.), Read Chapter Five: Transitioning the Performance Management System. (If you want to read one more relevant chapter, even though such a chapter will cover stuff that's a little beyond the people side of change, read Chapter Six which is all about using project management for transition (e.g., people) projects.

Option Three: I want everything, big picture down and the details!!

If that is your goal, just read the book straight through. Take in all the logical steps for "what to do, what not to do, and how to do each step" for successful organizational change. Readers will get all the goodies they need to be able to nail the many transition projects that must be completed for successful organizational change.

Special Bonus Option: I just want to read three pages, no more, and no less!!

We understand your pain … so we wrote the table of contents as the checklist for successful projects! (Start from Chapter Two)

ROBERT CUYLER, PHD AND DUTCH HOLLAND, PHD

PREFACE

The Promise and
State of Telemedicine

- *Telemedicine has been described as "The Next Big Thing" whose global market is predicted to grow six times in the next five years*

- *Telemedicine has a poor record of implementation and a very patchy history of adoption ...*

The Good News and the Bad News about Telemedicine

Telemedicine can be broadly defined as the delivery of healthcare at a distance by electronic telecommunications. The practice of telemedicine takes many forms, from the direct diagnosis and treatment of patients in remote / distant sites by doctors over video-conference to the automated home monitoring of patients with chronic health conditions. Despite decades of research and practice in the field, the widespread adoption of telemedicine is a work in progress.

Telemedicine has been described as "The Next Big Thing" whose global market is predicted to grow from $1 Billion in 2016 to $6 Billion in 2020 (The World Market for Telehealth – A Quantitative Market Assessment – 2011, InMedica). Others watching the field, however, maintain that "telemedicine has a poor record of implementation and a very patchy history of adoption, with a slow, uneven and fragmented uptake into the ongoing and routine operations of healthcare." (Zanaboni, P. & Wooten, R., BMC Medical Informatics and Decision Making 2012, 12:1). Great potential, distant reach, improved patient care ... what could be wrong?

The bottom line of this book is that implementation of telemedicine is a complex and under-estimated endeavor that has reduced what could be a great river of comprehensive medical services to a small stream or a trickle. The root cause of failures in implementing telemedicine is similar to that of other technology implementations. In the excitement and complexity of implementing the "gee whiz" technology, implementers frequently take their eyes off the ball and let their project succumb to unmitigated risks.

Figure P.1: The Three Categories of Implementation Risk

The problem(s) of implementation is the failure to identify and mitigate three fundamental kinds of interdependent risks as shown in the Figure P.1:

- **Technical Risks** … will the technology work as it is supposed to with the needed performance level and reliability?

- **Organizational Risks** … if the technology works, will the organization that hosts telemedicine use it widely and in a disciplined way?

- **Business Risks** … if the technology works, and organization members use it widely and in a disciplined way, will telemedicine not only enable good care but also positive business results?

ROBERT CUYLER, PHD AND DUTCH HOLLAND, PHD

The three risk categories are omnipresent in telemedicine implementation. However, strong and informed management can mitigate them and move their organizations forward to implementation success.

One of the challenges in coming to grips with the growth, adoption, effectiveness, and sustainability of telemedicine comes from an almost impossibly wide scope and breathtakingly rapid evolution of medical technology. Within the past decade, developments in telemedicine have accelerated due to the widespread deployment of fast internet bandwidth and the explosion of low cost devices and applications which carry the potential of delivering healthcare services. However, other aspects of healthcare technology remain significantly behind other industries. The technology disconnect may be starkly captured in healthcare systems that treat brain tumors with Gamma Knives but continue to struggle with the shift from paper charts to electronic medical records.

The bulk of telemedicine history rides on a foundation of grant and government supported initiatives, such as NASA's telemedicine programs in manned space flight, medical care to remote locations such as Arctic and Antarctic scientific stations, and large scale correctional health projects. Projects of this magnitude in essence defined the early and mid-stage trajectory of telemedicine, testing new technologies and establishing both case study and empirical analyses of outcomes, cost-effectiveness, and patient/physician satisfaction.

The Implementation of Telemedicine in Healthcare Organizations

In our experience providing consulting services to hospitals and healthcare organizations, we have frequently found conversations about telemedicine opportunities quickly turning to projects in the past that have not come to full fruition. The long list has included grant-supported programs whose funding has expired and not morphed into sustainable services. Purchased or grant-supplied telemedicine equipment may be gathering dust, seldom or never having been used for its intended purposes.

One challenge to the field is that, despite a substantial history, telemedicine still seems new and exotic. The ability to see a doctor on a screen who can examine, diagnose, and treat without being in the same room maintains a whiff of 'magic'. As the technological complexity and cost has shrunk, a piece of that 'magic' can be purchased very inexpensively as healthcare capital purchases go. Too often, equipment is put in place without understanding or planning for the many tasks that must be accomplished to provide medical care effectively. Unlike "Field of Dreams," if you build it, they might not come (and usually do not).

The list of culprits for failed telemedicine projects can be long and varied, but here are a few of the contenders we've encountered:

- Telemedicine services were not adequately recognized or reimbursed by insurers.
- Equipment was too hard to use.
- Picture or sound quality was poor.
- Doctors were too busy with other obligations or not interested in seeing patients over telemedicine.
- Doctors didn't believe that they could provide necessary quality of care over telemedicine.
- It was a great success when the original doctor who championed telemedicine was involved, but fell apart when he/she left.
- Scheduling was too complicated and inefficient.
- Access to necessary medical records was incomplete or too complicated.
- Staff were not trained well enough or were expected to "fit telemedicine into" their regular workday.
- The demand for services at the patient care side was not as large or predictable as expected.
- The services lost money because delivery of care was more expensive than expected and/or reimbursement/collections were less than expected.

The People Variables Have a Major Impact on Implementation

Everett Roger's landmark work on the diffusion of innovation provides useful concepts to introduce into the conversation on telemedicine implementation. Rogers conceptualizes the human side of technology adoption into five distinct personal styles, each of which will certainly appear in the course of a telemedicine project. These personal styles exist on a continuum, ranging from a high affinity to adopt a new technology at one extreme to a high propensity to resist adoption. It is vital to understand the perspective of each style and to factor their role, power, and influence into the organizational (or bi-organizational) landscape of the project. (Rogers, Everett M. (1983). *Diffusion of Innovations*. New York: Free Press.)

Innovators: These folks are the smallest segment of the population

ROBERT CUYLER, PHD AND DUTCH HOLLAND, PHD

but have the strongest passion for the new and innovative. They are typically the first to introduce new ideas within organizations, often after exhaustive research and tinkering. As new gadgets are catnip for Innovators, it is easy to imagine that the spark for telemedicine within an organization may originate here. The intense focus of the Innovators may blind them to essential practicalities, which may include external factors such as licensure or reimbursement policy or internal factors such as organizational constraints or politics.

Early Adopters: Early Adopters are keenly interested in finding innovation and leaping in before the mainstream is even aware. They are quick to see new opportunity and are invested in being trendsetters within their fields. They have less tunnel vision than innovators and are more likely to be seen as champions for new causes and approaches. Early Adopters may identify opportunities and solutions and may tweak innovations in ways that facilitate broader adoption.

Early Majority: This group is less awed by changes and innovation, but are responsive to the excitement and hype of the Early Adopters. At the same time, the Early Majority is much more sensitive to cost and risk as well as to ease of use. A more pragmatic streak dominates, creating a more realistic scan of the internal and external environment for the facilitating and hindering factors that accompany change.

Late Majority: Much more conservative on this end of the continuum, the Late Majority avoid risk and change and can readily anticipate what can go wrong. These individuals are averse to adopting technologies until they become the proven standard. They may be pulled along by a need to fit in with the Early Majority as change begins to consolidate within the organization. However, they may be readily swayed by the final group, the Laggards.

Laggards: These folks are the last to get comfortable with change and innovation and the most ready to identify the impending doom that the innovation will surely unleash. In organizational change processes, the Laggards may actively and loudly challenge new initiatives with finely honed arguments or may passively resist.

Caveat: We do not suggest nor believe that Roger's paradigm necessarily represents a one-dimensional personality style. It is possible that an individual responsible for regulatory compliance may function as a Late Majority or Laggard within a healthcare organization while living in the Early Adopter camp in regards to smart phone applications or ethnic menu choices for dinner. From a functional perspective, however, the key individuals within the organization will sort out within Roger's continuum as the telemedicine project unfolds, creating dynamics that need to be recognized and addressed in the course of the project.

It is common that telemedicine initiatives originate within organizations from the Innovator and Early Adopter side of the curve. The fate of the telemedicine project often hinges on the organizational role, power, and influence of these individuals. An initiative which gets started, as many often do, with Innovators and Early Adopters in mid-organization roles may have hugely different outcomes depending on the style of the organizational decision-makers. Having a CEO, CFO, or Chief Medical Officer in the Early Majority camp will play out very differently than an otherwise similar organization with Laggards in the final decision-making roles.

As we discuss organizational change, we will address the role of vision and the critical role of communicating that vision within the organization. The success of telemedicine implementation, no less than any other organizational change, will be highly dependent on the extent to which the key stakeholders embrace the vision and organizational commitment vital to the project and drive that organizational change forward. We are aware that the reader may potentially range from the CEO of a health system undertaking a fundamental change in the strategy of the organization to the techie Innovator who has invented or identified a new gadget which could transform a single procedure provided by a single specialty. We hope to introduce a conceptual framework and toolkit which can be relevant to either scenario.

The Technology Variables Have a Major Impact on Implementation

The cool technology of telemedicine can be the blessing or the curse in the wider adoption into mainstream medicine. For many of us, our first interactive videoconference demo sticks in the mind as a glimpse of a game-changing

ROBERT CUYLER, PHD AND DUTCH HOLLAND, PHD

technology. Unlike some other important technologies, telemedicine is easily graspable in the way that a new pacemaker lead is not. The equipment is tangible, relatively inexpensive, and easy to use. It is perhaps this seeming simplicity that leads too many organizations to undertake telemedicine projects without the detailed study of organizational culture and work processes, followed by systematic project management. What seems like such an easy-to-use, intuitive device can quickly begin to appear useless or worse if there are too few doctors or too few patients, if the process does not deliver real, quantifiable benefits to each side of the camera, if services are not paid for as expected, if the work processes on each side are not clearly established and codified, and the list goes on.

Telemedicine is an umbrella term for a wide variety of healthcare applications that may range from experimental to mainstream. Gartner's 'Hype Cycle' framework provides a useful concept for judging telemedicine applications in light of the organization's core mission and strategy. By articulating the factors and time frames involved in the mainstream adoption of specific telemedicine applications, Gartner's analysis can help organizations evaluate proposed medical technologies on the basis of a variety of factors, including the maturity of the technology, regulatory and reimbursement climate, evidence base for effectiveness, and infrastructure needs.

Gartner's 2012 analysis of telemedicine broadly characterizes the telemedicine space for Healthcare Delivery Organizations (HDOs) as follows:

> "HDOs must view telemedicine as a potential opportunity and must evaluate each telemedicine application for its relevance to their core mission or business. They should stop piloting and start deploying the most mature or promising telemedicine applications when the effectiveness of care is comparable to, or better than, the alternative; when cost savings can be expected; or when there is a clear business need. Government agencies responsible for healthcare delivery should encourage the use of telemedicine where appropriate. They must address the legal and regulatory obstacles to its use, and create incentives for healthcare payers to reimburse it. Healthcare payers should expand their coverage of the more-mature and higher-benefit telemedicine applications, and they may need to modify their reimbursement methodologies to allow for this.

Adoption of telemedicine applications will require the engineering of changes in care delivery processes to turn telemedicine into a routine tool for delivering healthcare and an integral part of care management services. Of all the success factors for telemedicine, this is the most important."

Gartner places a variety of telemedicine applications in a graphical representation that models applications from near science fiction to the mainstream. The graph below illustrates the model, with applications with an expected long time to mainstream to the left (representing emerging technologies such as robotic tele-surgery) to those at the right of the curve which have already become the standard of care (tele-radiology). One of the authors had the recent experience of helping his father install a bed-side device which automatically monitors his pacemaker/defibrillator and streams data to the manufacturer, a perfect example of a home-monitoring telemedicine application which has reached the Plateau of Productivity.

Figure P.2: The Technology Hype Cycle

An additional appeal of the Hype Cycle is that it not only captures the macro-environment of telemedicine applications in national healthcare, but also can address the micro-environment within an organization. The trajectory of

ROBERT CUYLER, PHD AND DUTCH HOLLAND, PHD

individual telemedicine projects in our experience mirrors the Gartner[1] graph in many cases, from the initial excitement of identifying a cutting edge medical technology to the peak of excitement as the stakeholders envision expanded markets, improved margins, better healthcare outcomes for distant patients and communities. As the realities of project implementation sink in, the project enters the trough of disillusionment where deadlines are missed and budgets revised. The fortunate projects survive with diminished dreams, while others crash and never approach the plateau of productivity. It is the authors intention to articulate a process by which organizations can approach telemedicine with a clear view of the purpose of the initiative within the organization's mission, identify the steps necessary to prepare for organizational change, and to implement the project ON TARGET, ON TIME, AND ON BUDGET.

A Valid, Comprehensive Model of Implementation is a Requirement

While a "people model" that describes innovators and laggards and a "technical model" that can explain the technology patterns are both valuable, they do not cover the complete domain of the implementation space. A model for implementation like the one explained in this book must cover the waterfront of needed actions, issues that need to be resolved, and above all, the variables behind the technical, organizational and business risks. Consider some of the complexities that must be describable by an implementation model.

> **Technology Myopia:** As noted above, the technology of telemedicine is tangible, affordable, and easy to demonstrate. It is all too easy for project planners to envision that having cameras available at the provider and patient sides of a health organization means that the system is telemedicine-ready, with little else to do except arrange for patients to be at one camera and a doctor at the other. Actually, telemedicine implementation is complex, with multiple infrastructure requirements necessary as well as full understanding of facilitating and complicating human variables.

---

1   Gartner, Inc., Hype Cycle for Telemedicine, 2012, Thomas J. Handler, M.D., July 23, 2012. Gartner does not endorse any vendor, product or service depicted in its research publications, and does not advise technology users to select only those vendors with the highest ratings. Gartner research publications consist of the opinions of Gartner's research organization and should not be construed as statements of fact. Gartner disclaims all warranties, expressed or implied, with respect to this research, including any warranties of merchantability or fitness for a particular purpose.

Origin within the Organization: In the authors' experience, many telemedicine projects do not place enough emphasis on the critical role of senior management and of physicians. Many projects emerge from non-physician middle managers such as hospital department heads who become aware of the potentially expanded horizons that telemedicine can facilitate. The idea may then be brought to the hospital's Information Technology group, who often have an affinity for new technology and perhaps some prior experience. Significant time, effort, and expense may be spent before determining if the project fits within the strategic vision of senior management.

Thin, Unrealistic Implementation Plans: Unschooled in project management, the telemedicine project team, frequently made up of middle managers, may launch the initiative without a detailed understanding of the resources necessary to implement or a full understanding of the broader involvement of related departments (billing, compliance, vendor technical support) and technologies (electronic medical record, scheduling) necessary to support telemedicine. Budgets are often unrealistic for both cost and revenue, which may then result in a "soft sell' to senior management in the early stages, only to risk loss or weakening of executive support when the true costs and time frames become apparent.

Lukewarm support from Senior Executives: Those senior executives, who are neither creating nor driving the needed organization vision and commitment, may provide lukewarm support for the project, which may fly under the executive's radar because the cost and complexity has been underestimated. When the project lacks full understanding and support of more senior management, the project champions often lack the real and perceived power and influence to commit the financial and human resources necessary to drive the organizational change process.

Inadequate Physician Involvement and Support: Doctors, on the other hand, are typically independent professionals on the medical staff of the organization or who may be employed by an affiliated but somewhat autonomous physician organization.

ROBERT CUYLER, PHD AND DUTCH HOLLAND, PHD

Regardless of organizational role, physicians also tend to be highly focused on independence, autonomy, and the ability to make fundamental decisions about the adoption of new medical procedures or technologies.

Nevertheless, many projects are designed with an assumption that doctors will come on board. Lack of input from key physicians is common, as they are notoriously hard to bring together for planning meetings. Projects may be well underway before the project leaders become aware that physician buy-in is lacking, jeopardizing the viability of the project. Another common scenario is that a single doctor (an Innovator or Early Adopter) will be fully supportive of the project, fueling the enthusiasm of the work group. Without input of all the physician stakeholders, the project may proceed, only to crash at a later date when the necessary physician support is unattainable.

> "Thus a crucial factor in the adoption of telemedicine is the attitude of the health professionals on the ground. Since most telemedicine applications require additional effort and technical expertise, the use of telemedicine is almost always more time and trouble than practicing in the ordinary way. We believe that before health professionals will seriously consider the use of telemedicine, there must be some personal advantage to the user, in addition to the general advantages to society." (Zanaboni, P., & Wooten, R., BMC Medical Informatics and Decision Making 2012, 12:1)

The Availability of Physicians: One perspective that telemedicine program architects sometimes fail to take into sufficient account is that many if not most physicians are already booked with full caseloads, if not waiting lists. Unless the availability of doctors is factored in to the earliest stages of planning, much effort can be expended before the critical ingredient of physician supply is discovered. Even when the physician supply is adequate, the buy-in of the doctors is essential, with consideration given to changes in office routine, work-flow, scheduling, comfort with new technology among critical variables. In our experience, the personal advantage to the physician must be significant, with facilitating factors including reducing or eliminating travel, opening new markets, increased payments, or increasing value to (and compensation from) a health system by offering specialist services or consultations that improve the health system's operations.

Asking Too Much from Telemedicine Champions: It is not uncommon for a key physician to initiate or join the initiative at an early stage and function as the 'telemedicine champion'. The organizational influence of a key physician can play a very important role in helping a telemedicine initiative "gain traction" with administration as well as with other physicians. Not surprisingly, the "telemedicine champion" often falls in the "Early Adopter" camp and is comfortable with new technologies and non-traditional approaches to medical practice.

While having the "champion" on board can give the early stages of a telemedicine project a boost, there are also some inherent risks in depending too heavily on this key physician. When the champion is a section chief or medical director who has the power and influence to introduce telemedicine to his or her peers and to re-shape delivery systems, adoption of telemedicine may be accelerated. On the other hand, when the champion is a staff physician without significant organizational power and influence or if the bulk of the medical staff are Late Majority or Laggards, project risks escalate. Some telemedicine projects falter when broader adoption by physicians does not occur or if the telemedicine champion leaves the organization.

In many ways, connecting a doctor and patient by videoconference is the easiest part of the telemedicine enterprise. Getting the patient scheduled with the physician, having staff adequately trained to present the patient and coordinate care, documenting care so that it is available to patient-side and doctor-side, and managing prescriptions are the real challenges that must be addressed by the implementation model.

ROBERT CUYLER, PHD AND DUTCH HOLLAND, PHD

Given the complexity of issues just described, it is clear that a robust, yet practical, implementation model will be needed to move the implementation success record upward. The model "previewed" in Figure P.3 will be at the heart of this book's explanation of implementation steps needed for success. An immediate reaction might be that the model is intimidating at best and pure gobble-de-gook at worst. Never fear, this book will reveal the power and the "elegant simplicity" of this tried and true model for implementation.

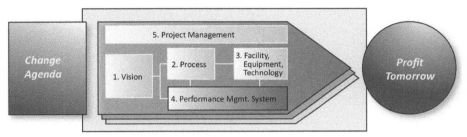

Figure P.3: Implementation steps needed for success

The Purpose of this Book

Telemedicine will not see anything close to its full potential for cost-effective patient care if the healthcare industry does not learn to effectively and efficiently implement telemedicine practices into service organizations.

It is the goal of the authors to detail the planning and organization necessary to implement telemedicine on target, on time, and on budget. We realize that by examining the process in such detail we may dissuade some hospitals, healthcare organizations, or doctors from even attempting telemedicine once they understand the magnitude of the undertaking. Similarly, we sometimes wonder if some couples would have babies if they really realized just how expensive, demanding, and exhausting it is to raise children.

Perhaps there are some projects which should not be implemented if the purpose and long-term viability of services is not sufficient, if organizational commitment is lukewarm, if work processes are not modified, or if adequate training is not provided. Failed telemedicine projects can drain resources which would be better directed elsewhere, not to mention perpetuating a concern that telemedicine is not ready for prime time.

The book is aimed at the healthcare leaders, managers and technical professionals who have the opportunity and/or the responsibility of taking a

Telemedicine Project from the conceptual stage all the way to a working reality that is economically thriving.

The book is not light reading ... because it is focused on the "how to's" of implementation of telemedicine in a real-world organization, a complex and time consuming task. The important point about this book is that it contains a valid, proven, effective formula for implementing a major organizational change like the one needed to add a telemedicine practice. This book does not have all the answers for implementation because each situation is unique ... but the book does have enough "strong bones" to be a valuable base for effective and efficient implementation.

ROBERT CUYLER, PHD AND DUTCH HOLLAND, PHD

Successful Organizational Change

Today's leaders must be able to
- *Run the business well ... all the time and*
- *Change the business well ... every time.*

The Management Imperative to Lead Change ... and Change Projects

Organizational change is happening in almost every healthcare organization but success has been elusive. Senior leaders in healthcare know that changes are needed not only system-wide but in their own organizations. They know the kinds of changes their organizations need and when they are needed. And certainly they know that the responsibility for change rests squarely on their shoulders. Many changes in healthcare are associated with the introduction of new technologies like telemedicine. Such an introduction requires an organizational change.

Implementation of Telemedicine is not a technical exercise; Telemedicine requires a successful organizational change.

Healthcare executives know that their boards of directors expect more than day-to-day performance; those board members expect the executives they support to make the changes needed to ensure a profitable, long-term, future for the organization. In short, today's healthcare leaders must both run the business well all the time and change the business well every time.

Changing the way an organization works is no longer an occasional exercise;

change is no longer the exception ... it is now the rule. Introduction of new technology like telemedicine is now the rule, not the exception. Changing the way an organization operates with new technology is central to organizational improvement and to the enhancement of business or organizational results. In today's world, change management that can handle technology introduction is the most important role of organizational leadership.

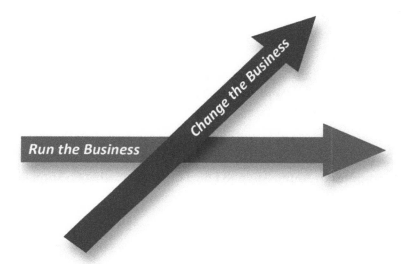

Figure F.1: Run the Business, Change the Business

The paramount problem with organizational change in general is that change initiatives are frequently unsuccessful. The often-quoted statistic is that only 30% of organizational change attempts meet management expectations of transitioning the organization from one way of doing business to another. While telemedicine success rates are not available, anecdotal evidence suggests a similar low success rate. Four reasons for poor change performance are apparent. Today's healthcare leaders may lack:

1. **A change-the-business mind set**. A key reason that change projects fail is because the managers who lead them lack both a change-the-business mindset and a change-the-business skill set. Most managers have spent the majority of their careers running a business, not changing one, and consequently they lack the knowledge and the experience needed to lead organizational change successfully.

2. **Appreciation for and competence in Project management:** Managers

ROBERT CUYLER, PHD AND DUTCH HOLLAND, PHD

who spend their careers running a business do not develop skills or experience in project management thinking or use. Consequently many organizational changes are not treated like projects with fixed beginnings or ends, or, at the other extreme, change initiatives are treated as projects but chartered with unmanageable scope or complexity.

3. **Awareness that a technology implementation is a business initiative:** First and foremost, implementing telemedicine is a patient service and business initiative, not a technology project. Many implementing a telemedicine practice do not clarify the need to look beyond the technology being implemented to the business reason for implementation. Many implanting telemedicine also do not understand the need to prepare the organization for use of the technology in the workplace.

4. **An understanding of the formula for organizational change:** The management community as a whole lacks an understanding of the moving parts that make up an organization, moving parts that must be managed in order for successful change to happen. Change projects like implementing telemedicine are not easy to understand or manage ... what is needed is a universal understanding of ways to successfully complete change projects. In short, most managers lack an understanding of the formula for organizational change.

These four issues must be addressed in change management literature as well as in the minds of today's healthcare leaders, or organizations will continue to flounder under the waves of change confronting them. A goal of this book is to resolve all four issues.

Implementing Telemedicine Requires an Organizational Change

A common and sometimes useful way of thinking about introducing a new way of thinking and acting in an organization is shown in Figure F.2. While Figure F.2 clearly communicates that implementing a telemedicine practice is the goal, the diagram itself tends to focus thinking on the definition and explanation of the contents of telemedicine. Implementers who have that view below tend to construct their implementation road map almost exclusively of communication and intensive training on telemedicine concepts, technology and techniques ... which turn out to be inadequate steps for the full integration of a telemedicine practice into a healthcare organization.

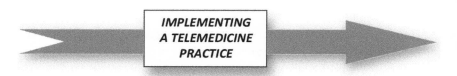

Figure F.2: Focusing Attention on the "Contents of Telemedicine"

The central idea in organizational change is to take an organization that is operating in one way (without the targeted technology) and to transition that organization to a new way of operating that includes the targeted technology (Figure F.3). That is, the bottom line task is taking an organization that is operating without a telemedicine practice and changing it to become an organization that has telemedicine as one of its ways of caring for patients. It really is as simple as that … and as complex too, because organizations have many "moving parts" that will be involved in any transition to a different way of doing business.

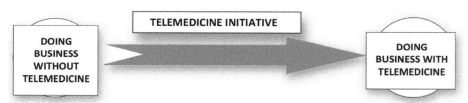

Figure F.3: Focusing Attention on the Organizational
Change Needed to Implement Telemedicine

The starting place for transitioning an organization to a different way of doing business is with the understanding of what an organization is and what organizational change means. We are not implying that people who work in today's healthcare organizations don't understand them — of course they do — to the level needed to do a good job of running their day-to-day business. But we have found that most managers and employees do not understand organizations at the level needed to lead effective organizational change. It would be hard to say that I don't understand my car; I drive it to work every day, I ensure that it's taken care of; I even play with it occasionally on a deserted winding road. Of course I understand it — as a transportation system or a toy. But the truth is that I don't understand very much about my car as a system of moving parts. I've always counted on somebody else to keep it running.

Managing change requires us to know something about what an organization is from a structural or systems point of view. We need to learn something about the many moving parts of organizations — like a driver would have to learn some

ROBERT CUYLER, PHD AND DUTCH HOLLAND, PHD

mechanical information if he had to take over responsibility for maintaining his car. In today's world of work, where healthcare managers must be able to both run the organization to get today's business done and to change the organization so that it will be ready to do tomorrow's business as well, knowledge of the moving parts of an organization is indispensable.

The way any organization works at a given point in time is the direct and inescapable result of the configuration of its moving parts. An organization has four main components or categories of moving parts that are vitally involved in every change in its way of doing business.

1. **Vision** ... the organization's sense of what it is, where it is trying to go, and how it intends to get there, as in its "business model" ... the unifying idea that is the organization's identity.

2. **Work processes** ... the many steps that organization members must take on a daily basis to satisfactorily produce the organization's products and/or serve its patients.

3. **Facilities, equipment, and technology (FET)** ... the organization's facilities along with its technologies, tools, equipment and software, that organization members use to do the work of the organization.

4. **Performance management system** ... the organization's mechanism for engaging workers to follow work processes, using the provided tools and technologies to enact its vision.[2]

---

2   The moving parts of an organization have been identified by no less than a veritable "who's who of OD" serving as the Board of Editors of the widely-accepted Jossey-Bass / Pfeiffer series of books on Organization Development: David Bradford is senior lecturer in Organizational Behavior, Graduate School of Business, Stanford University; W. Warner Burke is Professor of Psychology, Columbia University; Edith Whitfield Seashore is organizational consultant and co-founder of AUNTL Masters Program in Organization Development; Robert Tannenbaum is emeritus Professor of Development of Human Systems, University of California, Los Angeles; Christopher G. Worley, Director of the MSOD Program at Pepperdine University; and Shaolin Zhang is senior member of Organization Development for Motorola (China) Electronics Ltd.

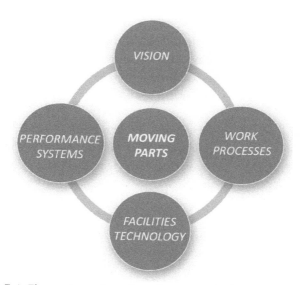

Figure F.4: The major categories of an organization's moving parts

An organization cannot change from one way of doing business to another without changes in its moving parts. Organizational change requires physical alteration of these four components or there will be no change at all. Calling these needed alterations "requirements" may help managers see that the needed alterations of an organization's moving parts are not optional; they are requirements!

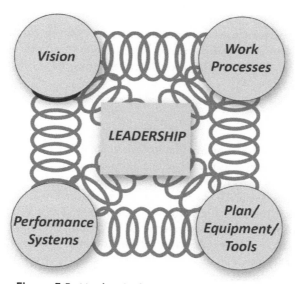

Figure F.5: Mechanical parts of an organization

ROBERT CUYLER, PHD AND DUTCH HOLLAND, PHD

> ### Successful Organizational Change
>
> *Successful organizational change, i.e., moving from one way of doing business to another, depends on the use of the change formula made up of the following "moving parts" ...*
>
> 1. *communicating a new and exciting vision,*
> 2. *creatively altering work processes,*
> 3. *incorporating robust and powerful FET, and*
> 4. *re-structuring challenging roles for employees.*
>
> *Successful change also depends on the use of disciplined project management that ensures that all the organization's moving parts are prepared and positioned properly for a new and better way of doing business.*

These four alterations make up what we call the requirements for a successful transition from one way of operating to another. We also see the list of moving parts as a sort of "formula for organizational change." Attempting organizational change without a new vision or without altering any of the other three moving parts will result in a contribution to the "70%" statistic of change attempts that do not meet management expectations.

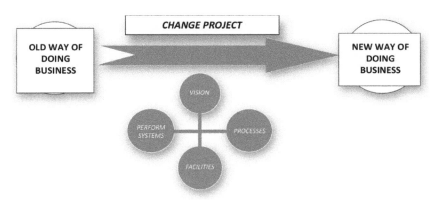

Figure F.6: Organizational change as a project

Understanding organizational change as a series of change projects

The old question asks, "How do you eat an elephant?" And the answer follows, "One bite at a time!" And how do you change an organization? One project at a time. Changing an organization is a big job and trying to make the change as one single initiative is just too general to be manageable. Successful organizational change depends on the completion of several well-thought-out change projects that, when completed, will have produced the new way of doing business.

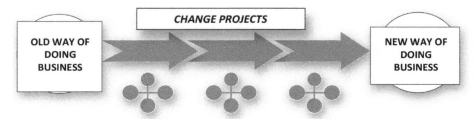

Figure F.7: Organizational change as a series of projects

The formula for each of the change projects is a fractal of the formula for changing the entire organization. That is each change project requires the use of the same actions in the general formula as shown in Figure F.7 above. The scope of these "smaller change projects" will not cover as much ground as for an entire organizational change and therefore can be easier to manage and successfully complete.

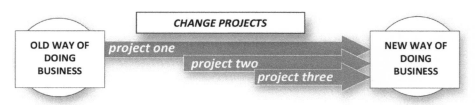

Figure F.8: Organizational change as a series of parallel projects

Identifying the change projects that will drive the organizational change

Imagine a medium-sized regional hospital that decides to change its business strategy and become the regional center for cancer treatment for its geographical area. Making this change would clearly give the hospital a new identity and image in the community … and require many dollars and a lot of resources. Imagine that a savvy executive team decides to manage the implementation of the new strategy with a set of change projects rather than as one massive initiative.

This example is so simple that the potential change projects are practically obvious. But for the sake of the example, imagine the executives using the organizational change formula as a guide to developing the first set of change projects.

ROBERT CUYLER, PHD AND DUTCH HOLLAND, PHD

Formula Elements	Change Projects
• **Communicate the vision**	• **Identity Project:** Marketing, Public Relations, and internal communication
• **Alter work processes**	• **Scheduling Project:** Altering the automated scheduling system to accommodate chemo
• **Alter FET** (facilities, tools, etc.)	• **Radiology Project:** Addition of radiology facility and equipment • **Pharmacy Project:** Adding to pharmacy the capacity to handle chemo
• **Alter performance management**	• **Project:** Attracting and integrating physicians into a cancer treatment practice • **Cancer Prevention Project**: Attracting and integrating professionals into a cancer prevention practice

This example shows quite a few change projects that could be generated after some careful thought. This list of six projects might be more than the regional hospital can successfully complete in a year's time, and it will be up to the executive team to select what they believe will be a full slate of projects for an upcoming time period (i.e., quarter or year). We urge change leaders to include only a few projects in their change list, projects that can be done well rather than many projects that can drag on, or be, marginally successful.

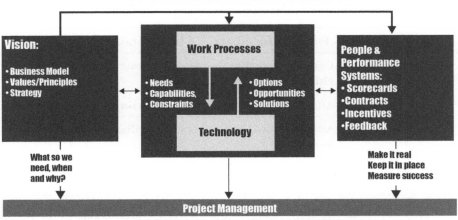

Figure F.9: The moving parts of organizational change

Identifying the change projects within the change projects

So now that we have identified the slate of change projects for the upcoming time period, what do we do next? Once again the same organizational change formula must be used, but this time the formula must be applied to each and every project. That's right, the same formula works at the project level as well as the organizational level.

The figure below shows the formula again in use for two of the six example change projects the regional hospital has elected to pursue for the upcoming year. As an example, two visions would be communicated to the radiology staff: the overall hospital vision of becoming a regional cancer center and the vision of how the radiology practice will be operating at the future target date. Work processes would also need to be considered at two levels: at the hospital level where we understand radiology to fit in a cancer center, and at the project level where we consider work processes inside a radiology department.

Change Project	Formula Elements	Radiology Change Projects
Radiology Project	Communicate the vision	Communicate the radiology vision
	Alter work processes	Acquire radiology clinical pathway info
	Alter FET (facilities, tools)	Purchase and install radiology assets
	Alter performance management	Identify radiology staff needs and hire needed physicians/technicians

Change Project	Formula Elements	Chemo Training Sub-Projects
Chemo Training Project	Communicate the vision	Communicate the chemo nursing vision
	Alter work processes	Amend nursing procedure manual
	Alter FET (facilities, tools)	Install sterilization facility
	Alter performance management	Purchase vendor training for nursing

Notice how "projects beget projects" as action plans are developed for a

ROBERT CUYLER, PHD AND DUTCH HOLLAND, PHD

desired change at both the organizational and project levels. At this point, the magnitude of moving parts in an organizational change can be seen more clearly ... along with some of the reasons why 70% of change projects come up short. The need for project management of the moving parts is now apparent.

The use of projects with strong project management has saved many organizational change initiatives. Project management based on generally-accepted principles will be invaluable in an organizational change like the one in our example. By focusing on completing four or five concrete change projects in a year's time, busy executives will know they are making progress toward the organization's vision for the future. Organizational change can be overwhelming in both complexity and scope. Our project-based approach can bring successful organizational change.

> *Now what is the point again?*
>
> *Nail each telemedicine change project, and you will have successful organizational change. Fail to nail each project ... and success goes out the window!*

This book and how it might be used

This book on changing or transitioning organizations to a new way of operating is all about doing organizational change right – and doing it at a mastery level. This book is not about the psychological concepts and theories that underlie organizational change,[3] it's about the real-world practical actions that must be taken to make organizational change work really well.

Where do these practical actions come from? They come from the many things learned over time about leading an organizational change; from the literature of management, change, and the behavioral sciences; from the principles of project management, from the lessons learned in the real world of organizational change. These practical actions come from those organizations that have mastered change and that have demonstrated time and again that they

---

3   While psychological concepts and theories that underlie organizational change will not be discussed explicitly in this book's content, you can know that such concepts have been "baked into" the actions recommended in the book.

can transition their organizations to new ways of working — on target, on time, and on budget!

The list of action steps in this book that are designed to impact the moving parts of an organization can be used as tasks in the project master schedule. A change professional might use this book for its "management and business language" that bridges today's world of business and many behavioral and change concepts. The book might be used to give to managers as a part of a change professional's explanation of how a change project might need to work. And last but not least, the information contained in this book about team composition, meeting agendas, and management scripts might assist a manager or a change professional in planning his/her change work.

As a reader of this book you will learn to guide change — a subject that has not likely been a part of your business education. You will no longer feel lost during organizational change — you will have a road map for change that you can confidently follow. You will know what concrete actions to take and when to take them. You will know what to expect of employees and how to work with them during the change process. You will be able to manage and communicate organizational change in a way that does not seem life- or ego-threatening for organization members.

Best of all, as a reader of this book, you will never again look at organizational change as a mysterious experience to be feared and fought. You will see organizational change as a set of concrete projects, creative acts of leadership than can be completed — on target, on time, and on budget!

Summary

In this day and time, American healthcare organizations from providers to payer systems are being forced to effectively change faster than they ever have before. In the past hospitals and health systems could gradually adapt to external forces that affected their bottom line. They could simply squeeze out waste, reduce unprofitable services and get by. But in today's world, the magnitude and speed of changing rules won't allow traditional gradual change techniques to be effective. Today's leaders must be able to run the business well all the time and change the business well every time.

ROBERT CUYLER, PHD AND DUTCH HOLLAND, PHD

So the one-paragraph summary of this book might be as follows: this is a book about making organizational change happen successfully in moving an organization from doing business without telemedicine to doing business with telemedicine by altering an organization's moving parts. Disciplined project management along with use of the change formula for altering the moving parts can lead to successful implementation of telemedicine, while ignoring any part of the formula puts an implementation at risk.

CHAPTER ONE

Introduction to Organizational Change Management

> *Mind-Clearing Example – Imagine a theater Director who works with the Producer to select the next new play, who then announces the new play to the cast, and says, "I'm going on vacation. I will be back for opening night!" The Director then says to the Producer, "You see, I just direct on-going performances; I don't shut down old plays and I certainly don't go through all that crap it takes to open a new one."*

The leader's job is to guide organizational change

LEADERS AND MANAGERS are hired to both run and change organizations. They are hired to run their organizations by today's rules in order to achieve today's target goals, and, at the same time, they are hired to prepare their organizations to run by new rules to be profitable tomorrow. Leaders are hired to cause change to happen ... on target, on time and on budget. In this book, we will treat "leading/managing change" as a proactive responsibility of every manager.

Effective organizational change is a transition challenge. Organizational change is most effective and efficient when attacked with specific actions that are based on proven bodies of knowledge. We will use the term transitioning to make a key point: changing an organization requires known concrete steps that alter the way the organization works today so that it will work differently tomorrow. We mean that transitioning a healthcare organization to operate with a telemedicine practice requires known, concrete steps. But first we need to understand an organization in a new way.

A universal metaphor for understanding organizational change

We have had very good luck in using metaphors and analogies to communicate about change with managers and students as well. We searched for years to find a simple metaphor for organizational change, and we finally found one ... one that was right under our noses all the time. The idea that an organization can be thought of as a "continuous one-act play performed by a theatre company" is used throughout the book.

The idea of vision, for example, can be characterized as a "script for a play." And the idea of organizational change can be likened to a theatre company transitioning to a new play. Vision – script, get it? Well, of course, everybody gets it ... and more. We all know that a play has a script (vision), roles (work processes), costumes/settings (tools), and actor contracts (performance agreements), rehearsals (training) and so on. The beauty of this theater metaphor is that almost everybody is familiar with the workings of a play. They already know that a script is needed, roles must be assigned, costumes must be fitted, contracts re-written and signed, etc.

Once the ideas of changing the play and changing an organization are "connected" in the minds of managers, the needed steps for organizational transition are very easy to explain and therefore, to plan. Since all world cultures have the concept of theatre imbedded in them, we have been able to use the theatre concept wherever we have worked.

In this book, we will use theater examples as a way of clearing the mind of organizational change "clutter" so that you can see how wrong some of the accepted organizational change practices are.

> *The guiding metaphor*
>
> *An organization can be thought of as a theater company that gives a satisfying performance to an audience of customers.*

Before discounting this metaphor as outlandish, consider that most of us get up each morning, put on our work clothes (costumes), travel to our company (the theater), walk into our office (the set) and execute our jobs (roles) according to the organizations' goals and objectives (the script) to deliver products and/

ROBERT CUYLER, PHD AND DUTCH HOLLAND, PHD

or services to customers (the audience) — until it's time to go home to start all over again the next day.

Once the theater metaphor is mastered, it becomes easy to understand a critically important concept in organizational change — that organizations can be seen as structured systems with concrete components or moving parts that must work and change together.

Using the theater metaphor, we can more clearly see and understanding an organization's four primary structural components

- **Vision ... like the storyline and script of a play.** The vision is the organization's sense of what it is and where it is trying to go, as in its business model

- **Work processes ... like the roles in the play.** Work processes are the steps that organization members must take on a daily basis to produce the organization's products and services

- **FET ... like costumes and sets.** FET includes the organization's facilities along with tools, equipment, and software. Workers use the organization's FET to enable work processes

- **Performance management system ... like the actors' contracts and rehearsals.** The performance management system is the organization's mechanism for engaging workers to follow work processes, using the provided FET to bring the organization's vision to life.

While it is easy to comprehend the connection of vision and script, or work processes and roles, it does take some stretch to see that the "agreements for performance," like actor contracts, are an attribute of the organization and not the employees/actors themselves.

In our experience, the most difficult part of organizational change for many companies is seeing that change is designed to alter the roles that people play in the organization, not to attempt to alter people themselves. In our experience, failure to grasp the idea that change hinges on altering roles and subsequent performance agreements that are made with employees is the most common cause of unsuccessful organizational change.

Understanding organizational change as "changing the play"

In the theater metaphor, organizational **change** would be the equivalent of a theater company transitioning from the daily performance of an existing play to the daily performance of a new play, requiring the physical transition of actor roles, costumes, sets, etc.

Imagine a theater company, with a dwindling audience for their current performance of "Romeo and Juliet," who decides to make the move to a fresh, contemporary version of "My Fair Lady." The transition to the new play requires many concrete steps to physically alter the script, roles, costumes and set as well as the specific contracts of the actors ... and that's all there is to it ... except for a million other details needed to shut down an award-winning play and replace it with another award-winner.

In the theater, change mastery is critical because no play lasts forever, and the success of the theater company will be determined by its ability to transition from one successful play to another. The same is true in healthcare where no way of operating will last forever, and the long-term survival of the organization will be dependent on making effective transitions over time.

Both managers and employees easily grasp the changes needed to transition a theater company from one performance to another — from learning new scripts and parts to changing costumes and sets, all the way to the full dress rehearsals before opening night. Once this theater metaphor is learned, managers can easily use it to understand why many organizational changes they have seen went awry!

Using the theatre metaphor to understand the formula for change

Using the idea of theater to guide our understanding of an organizational change, let's preview the five requirements to be covered in detail in the rest of the book. There requirements comprise what we think of as the "formula" for organizational change – the steps that must be followed to either "change from one play to another" or "change an organization from one way of doing business to another."

ROBERT CUYLER, PHD AND DUTCH HOLLAND, PHD

- **Requirement One: Communicate a vision for the organization**

> - *If you want to change the play, you must start by selecting and communicating a new script.*
>
> - *If you want to change an organization from one way of operating to another, you must start by communicating a new vision of how the organization should be operating at some selected future time.*

We have probably all been to a movie or theater production and come out with the evaluation that "the plot was weak" or even "there was no plot!" What we usually mean by that evaluation is that for us the production did not make sense and there was limited attractiveness, fun, or satisfaction. The production just didn't work for us.

Organizations also have a "story line or plot" that gets executed by the people in the organization. Sometimes it is a good story line (Windows software or Apple's iPAD) and sometimes it is not (the New Coke). Organizations use different words or terms to describe their story lines or plots. Story lines are called many things: Vision, Mission, Purpose, Strategy, Game plan, Direction … or any one of a dozen other terms. The hottest new title for an organization's story line is the mind twister … "Value Proposition!"

Our position is simple, we don't care what an organization calls its story line … it is just critical that the organization have one … and that everyone knows what it is! Our interest and idea is again simple; when an organization wants to change, one of the four things it will need to modify or alter is its story line, or its vision, the word we have elected to use in this book.

In a theater production, detailed written scripts are used … from which actors could read or conclude the story line. In organizations, much of the story line is not written down for everybody to read. Even in those cases where the organization has a written and posted mission, vision, and/or strategy, much of the story line is implicit … understood by many but not written down. In later sections of this book, we will make recommendations about making more of the organization's story line explicit to support organizational transitions. The bottom line is this; if we want the world to see a different story line from our organization (i.e., with a telemedicine practice), we will need to develop and detail that new story line ... or we will have nothing to use as a target for an organizational change.

- **Requirement Two: Alter work processes**

> - *If you want to change the play, you must identify and assign the roles called for in the new script.*
>
> - *If you want to change an organization, you must alter the work processes of the organization so that they work as needed for the new way of doing business.*

Theatergoers can easily identify parts or roles in a play because different actors do different things on stage. That is, each actor is seen taking certain steps, saying certain lines, hiding his derringer up his shirt sleeve, interacting with other actors in certain scenes. And if the theatergoer were to return to the theater some months later, she would likely see actors performing those same roles all over again (the actors might have changed but roles would not). In organizational terms, the parts that employees play are the daily work processes that produce the organization's goods and services.

An observer could follow different workers in an organization to see or even document the steps taken by that worker over the course of a time cycle (a work day, week, or month). Following all the workers in an organization could theoretically allow the observer to see all of the organization's work processes. An observer who sees all of an organization's work processes is likely to conclude, in a well-managed organization, at least, that all the processes seem to be focused on bringing about the purpose of the organization.

In fact, the kind of results that are produced by any organization at a given point in time are directly related to both the kind and performance level of all of the organization's work processes. So, from an organizational change perspective, if we want customers to experience a different story line from our organization, we will need to modify or alter our organization's work processes ... or the customers will see nothing different at!!

ROBERT CUYLER, PHD AND DUTCH HOLLAND, PHD

- **Requirement Three: Alter facilities, equipment and technology (FET)**

> - *If you want to transition to a new play, you must select the theater, build the props, and fit costumes for the actors.*
>
> - *If you want to transition a healthcare organization, old equipment must be altered and/or new equipment must be bought to enable the organization's new work processes.*

Theatergoers see props and costumes when they go to a performance. They don't see all of the theater or the "behind-the-scenes equipment," but they know they are there based on what happens on the stage ... scenes change, actors dangle, or dance into and out of rooms that were not on stage in the last scene. For many plays to make sense to the audience, certain props or costumes are needed. Imagine for a moment that a "fresh behind the ears" director decides to perform "Cats" with both male and female actors wearing business suits (or scuba gear)! While props and costumes don't "make the play," they clearly are indispensable parts of the whole ... and the clarity of the story line would suffer without them.

Just as in the theater, organizations require the use of FET to execute the work processes needed to produce the products and services that fulfill the organization's purpose or direction. For the sake of brevity we will use the word "FET" to represent the facilities, plants, equipment, tools, computer systems, the organization uses to do its day-to-day work. As an example, a local orthopedic radiology shop uses an office building, furnishings, x-ray equipment, stands for patients to stand on or beds for them to lie on, and computer hardware and software to bring to life its work processes and to make possible the development and testing of its primary product ... visible images for physicians to read.

And just as in the theater, some of an organization's FET is visible ... and some is, for all intents and purposes, invisible. Invisible tools include "what's behind the walls, under the floor, and in the ceiling" as well as what's inside the computer. Software turns out to be an indispensable tool in today's healthcare organizations, and software is, to a large degree, invisible to workers except for what they see on their computer screens. Months of alterations of an inventory control system can go along un-noticed while major alterations to the positioning of x-ray equipment would be hard to miss. For an organization to change the way it does business through its work processes, the organization's FET must be altered, whether it be visible or invisible.

- **Requirement Four: Alter performance systems**

> - *If you want to change the play, you must put actors under contract for the new play and rehearse them until they can perform their roles perfectly.*
>
> - *If you want to change an organization, workers must be under agreement to perform to altered, detailed job descriptions and goals, and workers must be trained in the new or altered work processes and accompanying FET.*

We clearly see the actors when we sit in the theater. It is the actors who bring the story line of the play to life. But what we see is the performance given by the actors. We know as we sit in the theater that the person we are see onstage is a professional actor portraying her role and speaking her lines from the script. We also know that the actor is under contract to do the play (or she would not be there!), and that the performance we are seeing is only possible after the actor studies and rehearses her part.

We see workers in organizations as actors with assigned parts who are under an agreement to give a performance for their organization. We see the training that the worker has received as akin to the study and rehearsal done by the actor to be able to perform in a play. The workers in our example radiology practice have been trained and certified in different roles in the organization – like radiologist assistants (RAs), nurse practitioners (NPs), radiology practitioner assistants (RPAs), – using the tools of the practice, to produce images for the physicians who request them.

The concrete, moving parts of the organization that we use in transition projects are worker agreements and training. We call these moving parts the "performance management system" that leaders of an organization use to ensure that workers will be ready, willing, and able to complete all the needed work for organizational success. In the theater, for example, the performance management system would be similar … with specific contracts for actors (calling for rehearsals

ROBERT CUYLER, PHD AND DUTCH HOLLAND, PHD

and performance in an assigned role for a certain amount of compensation) and planned rehearsals to ensure that the actors had developed their parts and were able to perform as required with the entire theatre company.

Beyond the worker agreement, the actor receives direction from the Director on some of the finer points of his performance of the part. The Director has the responsibility to tell the story in the play through the performance of the actors. And the actors have the responsibility to act the part to the best of their ability to ensure a successful performance. In organizations, workers have the responsibility to act out their assigned roles with the assistance of a manager who is responsible for blending a number of roles into the performance needed to meet her organizational goals.

- **Requirement Five: Manage the change as a project**

> - *If you want to transition to a new play, you must manage all the "moving parts" of the transition as a project: closely following a master schedule for handing out the script, for signing actors, for fitting costumes, for conducting rehearsals, and so on.*
>
> - *If you want to transition an organization to a new way of doing business with telemedicine as a core practice, the alterations of all moving parts should be treated as a project: closely following a schedule for communicating the vision, altering work processes, onboarding new telemedicine technology, training workers and so on.*

Even though actors are clear on the new play they are planning to perform, they need a day-to-day transition plan and schedule to get ready to perform. And even though organizational workers are clear on the vision that is to be implemented, they too need day-by-day or week-by-week action plans to guide them through the many steps of organizational change. Employees need an action plan that tells them "what to do on each Monday morning ..." to go forward with the coordinated implementation of the new vision.

These action plans must be a part of a critical path project management plan and master schedule that lays out all the transition work to be done for the organizational change. Critical to the action planning requirement is the translation of action plans on a weekly or monthly basis for all involved managers and employees so that they are clear on both their roles in transitioning to the new organization as well as playing a new or altered role in that new organization. Failure to keep action plans up to date and communicated would be like the director who does not lay out and communicate detailed plans and schedules for the reading for new roles, signing of contracts, fittings for new costumes, rigging of new props, dates for rehearsals, and so on.

The challenge in this project management requirement is to ensure that all of the required modifications to vision, work processes, FET and performance agreements have been completed in a thorough and comprehensive manner. While it may be a technical challenge to keep track of all of the needed alterations, particularly if the organization is large, it is technically not difficult to find out exactly where the organization is in organizational change.

You know where you are

Knowing where we are in transitioning a theater company to a new play or transitioning an organization to a new way of doing business is a matter of auditing the status of the change projects that have been established — and dealing with the reality of what we find:

- Either the vision for the company's new way of doing business with telemedicine has been developed and documented ... or it has not! Either the vision has been communicated to each manager and employee multiple times ... or it has not. Either managers have had the opportunity to discuss and question the new vision of a telemedicine practice and make it their own ... or they have not! Each member of the organization has been personally briefed on what will be the new way of working ... or he/she has not ... and so on.

- Either work processes have been altered ... or they have not! New procedures to allow people to follow those altered processes have been written and distributed ... or they have not! The old processes and their supporting procedures have been dismantled and destroyed ... or they have not!

- Either the new telemedicine FET is on board and working ... or it is not! Either the guidelines for operating the new FET have been written and

ROBERT CUYLER, PHD AND DUTCH HOLLAND, PHD

distributed ... or they have not. Either the old FET and its operating instructions have been removed and/or disabled ... or they have not!

- And either the performance agreement for each and every manager and employee impacted by the telemedicine practice has been altered and negotiated with him/her ... or it has not! Either each and every manager and employee has been trained on the new processes and new FET ... or they have not! And so on!!

Be ready for mind-clearing examples to introduce each chapter

In the chapters that follow, be on the look-out for "Mind-Clearing Examples." Such examples will be of a real-world situation that would be "absurd" to find in a theater company ... but that might be "common place" to find in the real world of business. For example:

> *Mind-Clearing Example – Imagine a Director who is communicating the new play to the theater company. He says, "Rather than give each of you that inch-thick script for the new play, look at this. I have prepared a couple of PowerPoint slides that will explain the entire play in a couple of minutes!"*

This would be an absurd idea in the theater ... and yet somehow it feels familiar in business as top management hands out the "ten key one-liners that describe their vision for the future." Such Mind-Clearing Examples will set the stage for the material to be covered in each of the chapters about transitioning an organization to a new way of doing business.

Introducing the example change projects

For the purposes of this book, emphasis will be placed on the implementation of telemedicine in healthcare organizations rather than on direct-to-consumer models. The focus will be on programs which are aimed at provision of health services, rather than primarily on research. Particular focus will be placed on organization-to-organization projects, which may encompass settings within the same healthcare family as well as those projects that link unrelated organizations. While technology implementation is challenging within an organization, the complexity escalates as the planning, coordination, and accountability of activities involves two organizations, often with significant differences in culture, vision, buy-in, and sophistication.

The nature of telemedicine projects often involves the delivery of services to remote, rural, resource-poor settings by larger, more complex healthcare organizations. Given these circumstances, it is not surprising that the implementation and subsequent delivery of services can be compromised by the complexity of the undertaking even in the best of circumstances. When projects are launched without the careful attention to design and project management advocated in this book, the results are all too often *OFF TARGET, LATE, AND OVER BUDGET.*

Two different examples will be used to illustrate the key actions in each of the following chapters. These examples should be considered "fiction based on truth." Both examples come from real-world organizational changes at the project level. Many of the small examples will read "more cleanly than reality" in order to illustrate key points. In actual fact, many of the small examples were very messy, clouded with organizational culture influences as well as organizational politics, both a part of the real world of organizational change but beyond the scope of the simple treatment in this book.

Example One: Telemedicine at Northwest Memorial Health Center

A health system consisting of a single large urban hospital and four small rural hospitals was having issues around the coordination of activities among the five facilities. The Northwest Memorial System had acquired two of the rural hospitals outright and had established long-term management agreements to lease and operate the remaining two hospitals from their hospital district owners. The additions to the health system had occurred over the past four years, and the integration of the formerly independent hospitals was a gradual and bumpy process.

During the transition, a competing health system acquired established primary care practices in three of the four rural service areas, and the Memorial system was experiencing an unexpected degree of out-migration from these communities

ROBERT CUYLER, PHD AND DUTCH HOLLAND, PHD

to the competing system. The Memorial CEO, in response, mobilized the executive team to study and address the lingering difficulties in integration of the hospitals and to develop strategic initiatives to protect market share and realize the intended gains of building a regional health system.

In initial meetings, the COO expressed concerns about the loss of surgical cases to the competing system. Patient satisfaction data showed significant concerns from patients about the need to travel to the hub hospital for pre-operative testing and pre-operative instructions that included visits with the surgeon and anesthesiologist. Travel time, parking expense, lost work time, and wait time to see the doctor were common complaints. The administrators of two of the rural hospitals pointed out the increasing numbers of psychiatric patients appearing in their Emergency Departments since the downsizing of a nearby state hospital and staffing shortages at the local community mental health center. Lengths of stay in the ED sometimes exceeded three days before a psychiatric bed could be found. Without access to behavioral health personnel, the ED physicians often relied heavily on sedating medications to manage agitated patients.

It was unclear how much of the acuity in the ED was a result of frustrated patients boarding in the ED for extended times and how much was a result of the psychiatric illness. The system ED Medical Director believed that some patients were sent to inpatient psychiatric beds rather than to community care simply because specialty consultation was not available to assess risk adequately in the ED. While an inpatient psychiatric unit was available at the urban North location, there was effectively no linkage among the five system hospitals for behavioral health.

The Chief Medical Officer sponsored a project named the Systems Specialty Integration Project to assess the specialty services available within the system to look at the coordination of care within the system, with a particular focus on identifying opportunities to use telemedicine to more effectively link the urban hub hospital and its specialists with the rural hospitals.

I. Pre-Op and Post-Op Surgical Telemedicine

A group of twenty-seven surgical procedures unavailable in the rural hospitals were identified as prime candidates for telemedicine. General surgical procedures available in the rural hospitals were specifically excluded in order to avoid diverting local cases and revenues to the hub hospital, which would undermine volumes and revenues at the rural hospitals. Cases would be referred by the local primary care physician, and a surgical nurse from the rural hospital would be trained to accompany and present the patient to the surgeon to discuss risks and benefits of the procedure and to obtain consents. Whenever possible, laboratory and imaging would be done at the rural hospital. In complex or high-risk procedures, an anesthesiologist would be available to meet prior to surgery.

Post-procedure consultations with the surgeon were also targeted as a potential for reducing travel demands on patients, as well as increasing compliance with recommended follow-ups. Spirited debate among surgeons about the safety of post-procedure consultations done by videoconference led to a decision to leave the decision of in-person versus telemedicine consultation to the discretion of the surgeon.

II. Emergency Psychiatry Consultations

The main North Memorial Hospital has the only psychiatric beds in the system, with adult and gero-psychiatric capacity. While the admitting psychiatrists share call for the inpatient units, they have never been willing to come to the Emergency Department for psychiatric consultations. Several years ago, Memorial Behavioral Health developed a mobile crisis team to respond to psychiatric cases at Memorial's ED as well as contracting to provide services to several other hospitals in the community. Staff social workers provide business-hour coverage while PRN staff handle evenings and weekends and are paid a contract rate for each assessment. These personnel assess patients for suitability of admission to the inpatient unit and can assist in placement for outpatient community care or involuntary hospitalization. Turnover is common, as the

ROBERT CUYLER, PHD AND DUTCH HOLLAND, PHD

role involves travel to multiple hospitals, which is particularly onerous during rush hours or evenings/weekends.

The rural hospitals have no psychiatrists on staff, and management of psychiatric emergencies is handled by Emergency Physicians who typically have discomfort with psychiatric emergencies. Limited assistance is given for psychiatric bed placement by the local community mental health centers. Frequency of psychiatric emergencies has increased significantly in the past three years, as has ED length of stay, sitter costs, and incidents such as staff injuries, AMA discharges, and elopements.

Telemedicine was identified as a potential means of distributing psychiatric assistance to the ED's in urban and rural hospitals. Opportunities were cited to improve the average daily census of North Memorial's inpatient psychiatric unit by improving access to Behavioral Health social workers, as well as potentially reducing ED length of stay, by linking the rural hospitals to the urban hub.

System ED doctors expressed great dissatisfaction with the refusal of the psychiatrists to provide consults in Emergency settings, contrasting that to greater cooperation from other specialties. The Psychiatric Section Chief defended the current practice and warned his medical colleagues that a requirement to travel to ED's for consults could result in some or most of his staff resigning their staff privileges, citing their unwillingness to travel in the middle of the night to see self-pay patients. Opportunities in private practice and employment options with no call responsibility were abundant, and doctors may well make 'quality of life' decisions that would end up destroying rather than improving access to care.

III. Cardiology

None of the rural hospitals have cardiologists on staff or in the community. Frequent re-admissions within 30 days for post-MI and congestive heart failure patients affected the hospitals' quality ratings and would in the near future affect revenue as

Medicare planned to penalize for high readmission rates. Lack of access to cardiologists was identified as a key ingredient in readmission rates, as was education on medication compliance and diet/exercise. The small hospitals saw little opportunity to recruit cardiologists to their medical staffs because of their rural location.

In the past, a visiting cardiologist held twice monthly clinics at two of the hospitals but discontinued because of the lost professional time and travel burden. The new system EMR promised easier remote access to medical records including labs and imaging. One of the North Memorial cardiologists had experience with cardiac telemedicine from a prior role with an academic medical center and expressed confidence in the quality of patient care when state of the art digital stethoscopes were available.

DID YOU NOTICE

1. *This case is ideal to illustrate the concepts in this book. What could be better than a centralized hospital will all the needed services surrounded by rural hospitals that cannot afford to have all their services in house?*

2. *But things are not as easy as they look as you will see as you follow Northwest to successes with its telemedicine practice.*

Example Two: Telemedicine at Medi-Tel

Dr. Ivan Janssen is an Emergency Medicine physician who left the military after seven years of practice in two war zones. He has vast experience in trauma care and cutting edge involvement with the latest technologies extending care to the most severe and dangerous environments. In his past two years, he has practiced in an academic medical center and completed an MBA. With his experience delivering care as well as designing and refining telemedicine

ROBERT CUYLER, PHD AND DUTCH HOLLAND, PHD

systems, Dr. Janssen believes that there are significant opportunities to bring specialty care to a variety of settings via telemedicine. Upon completing the MBA with its strong focus on entrepreneurship, he has begun to take steps to form a start-up company that would assemble a world-class group of specialty physicians to offer medical services to remote and high risk environments.

Having had the opportunity to review the latest medical technologies, Dr. Janssen believes that the core of the business can be operated using devices and technologies which have been designed, tested and FDA-approved by the inventor/manufacturer, rather than focus on inventing and developing new devices. As a medical services company rather than a hardware or software developer, Dr. Janssen realizes that intellectual property and patents are unlikely to develop as assets of the prospective company. Also, as a service provider, he wonders if the potential enterprise can scale effectively enough to develop a business with real growth potential and not function just as a boutique medical practice. Discussions with a select group of colleagues from his current academic medical setting as well as long-term colleagues finds a nucleus of interest among some of the doctors who are similarly interested in developing innovative models of care focused on distributing specialty care to remote and challenging environments.

A visit with one of Dr. Janssen's MBA professors results in an introduction to an angel investor who has led multiple start-ups in medical technology and has been part of funding several others. The 'angel' is impressed with Dr. J's history, credentials, and entrepreneurial spirit. He agrees to participate in a meeting with the other interested specialty physicians to explore the concept of a telemedicine business that would deliver medical care and expertise to distant locations.

Dr. Janssen lays out an initial concept, that of putting together a portfolio of elite physicians in a variety of specialties who would offer medical services via telemedicine. The physician group has detailed discussions of the kinds of specialties and services that would be suited to telemedicine, as well as the nature and availability of peripherals such as stethoscopes, examination cameras, and monitoring devices that would be needed to do remote care. As all of the physicians are currently busy in more traditional medical settings, there is clearly no real need to find patients or opportunities to keep them busy.

The 'angel' advisor stepped in to identify the key aspects of this potential new venture: The medical services would have to be a) interesting to the doctors, b) high quality medicine equivalent to ordinary face-to-face care, c) paid at high enough rates to merit the additional infrastructure needed to deliver telemedicine, d) capable of building an organization that had economic value beyond that of a traditional medical practice, and e) scalable in revenues and profits such that the enterprise could be an attractive acquisition target for some larger entity within five years.

The physician group agreed that these guiding principles made sense. In additional discussions, they identified emergency medicine, dermatology, cardiology, infectious disease, psychiatry, and neurology as specialties that had a potential good fit with telemedicine and would be of real value to remote environments. They further agreed that pursuing traditional health insurer reimbursement made no sense at this point, but that identification of organizations that had problems accessing medical care to personnel in challenging locations was the key to assessing viability of the prospective organization.

The group surmised that such organizations might be willing to pay a premium for medical care delivered to their remote locations. The 'angel' advisor suggested such organizations as oil companies, mining companies, or logistical support companies that sent personnel to war or conflict zones as potential customers. He agreed to start accessing his network to identify contacts in such industries or organizations who might have needs/interests in specialized medicine on demand.

When the doctors asked about how such a company might be launched, the 'angel' indicated that such a venture was right up his alley as well as raising funds from the doctors who would be involved, so that they would have skin in the game. He indicated that a detailed business plan was essential, including a thorough assessment of need and demand, potential customers, review of

ROBERT CUYLER, PHD AND DUTCH HOLLAND, PHD

competition, and financial forecasts. Dr. Janssen, fresh from his MBA, suggested that he and the 'angel' take the lead on developing a business plan. The 'angel' recommended that they stay away from venture capital financing at this time, as the company would need an operating business with track record. He also questioned whether venture funding made sense at all for a company that was not likely to own intellectual property or have massively scalable potential.

DID YOU NOTICE

This is another great case that is vastly different than Northwest. Imagine starting a telemedicine service company literally from scratch. Although the situations are vastly difference, you will see that the same change and implementation problems exist in this setting as well.

The great thing about the book is that it will treat both cases equally well ... guiding the organizations to the successful implementation of their telemedicine practices ... on target, on time, and on budget.

And now on to the chapters. Each of the following chapters will tackle one of the five key components of an organization, identifying the steps that will be needed to alter that component to allow the organization to transition to a new way of doing business.

INTRODUCTION
TO CHAPTERS TWO THROUGH SIX

The Recipe Format

Have you even noticed the format used for cooking recipes? First you see a list of ingredients. After that, you see the instructions for turning the separate ingredients into the dish. The idea is to explain the bits and pieces (the ingredients) before any attempt to explain how the bits and pieces will be combined.

We will follow a similar sequence for this book ... explaining the four major ingredients in some detail (communicate vision for telemedicine, alter processes for telemedicine, altering tools and technology, and altering the performance management system that will steer employees toward use of telemedicine). After those key chapters (Two through Five), you will read about the combining of ingredients for the integration of telemedicine into an organization in Chapter Six: Manage Change as a Project.

Got it? Ingredients first; then instructions on how to project-manage the ingredients for an organization that operates with a telemedicine practice. That sequence makes sense to us (and to chefs), but perhaps it might be more comfortable for many readers to look at a preview of the sequence.

The General Sequence

The general sequence of work to be managed in an organizational change project is as follows:

1. **Chartering the organizational change to telemedicine as a project:** The executive who is commissioning the organizational change should appoint a formal project manager and give him his first assignment of developing the formal charter for the telemedicine project. The project charter is the executive's and project manager's concise statement of the intent, goals, scope, change budget, limits of and responsibilities for the organizational change.

2. **Development, approval and communication of the master schedule:** The project manager sketches the beginning and desired end points of the organizational change, develops the task list, creates the first high-level master schedule, and seeks schedule approval by the executive in charge of the implementation of the telemedicine practice.

3. **Development of the vision and the case for organizational change:** The change leader launches those activities needed to develop in some detail the vision (i.e., the new way the organization will be doing business in the future with a telemedicine practice) as well as the case for change (why implement telemedicine, and why now?).

4. **Initial communication of the telemedicine vision and case for change:** The change leader begins the communication process designed to give the organization a heads-up to changes that are to be made along with the reasons for those changes.

5. **Identification of change work, that is, the alterations that will need to be made to accommodate a telemedicine practice:** The change leader names teams to identify needed alterations in

   - **Work processes**
   - **Facilities, Equipment, Tools (FET)**
   - **Performance management system** (e.g., worker roles, training, etc.)

6. **Development and communication of a detailed master schedule:** A detailed master schedule is created to show the calendar for completing all change work needed for the implementation of a telemedicine practice.

7. **Alteration of worker roles:** the change leader authorizes bosses to conduct one-on-one contracting with workers for

   - **Starting a new way of working** to support telemedicine at the targeted, change-over time
   - **Continuing to perform work** as it is currently done until change-over
   - **Completing the change work** required for change over (e.g., participating in training, new role development, new equipment break-in, etc.)

ROBERT CUYLER, PHD AND DUTCH HOLLAND, PHD

8. **Conducting change work:** Many consider this step as the heart of organization change, where existing work processes are studied, re-designed, and then altered to fit the change vision; where FET is analyzed and actions taken to modify it or to buy and install new FET; and where roles are altered and training delivered, and so on. This step alone can take weeks to months of hard work for some organization members while other members are uninvolved, continuing to conduct today's business as usual ... until that first training class appears on their schedules.

9. **Verifying all change work:** The change leader ensures all the needed change work has been done, including alteration of work processes, FET, and roles ... and that tests have been conducted to ensure that all needed alterations have been adequately made.

10. **Changing over to the new way of doing business:** At a specific time the various parts of the organization make the switch from doing work the old way to doing work the new way – with a telemedicine practice.

11. **Break-in (or learning curve phase) and stabilization:** The change leader aggressively leads during the first few weeks/months of the telemedicine practice, during which the organization continues to learn and make further refinements to work processes, FET, and worker roles to achieve the desired level of service.

So much for the preview and now on to the first of the ingredients chapters: Communicate the Vision of a Telemedicine Practice.

CHAPTER TWO

Communicate a Clear
Vision for Telemedicine

Mind-Clearing Example – Imagine a theater Director who works with the Producer to select the next new play ... but who then fails to communicate the selection to the theatre company. Imagine the company of actors receiving its only information about a possible new play from backstage gossip that says, "It's going to be a comedy ... starting in the fall ... we think!"

Construct the detailed vision for organizational change

REQUIREMENT ONE, A reasonable place to start, calls for leaders to construct and fully communicate a clear, detailed vision of the organization as they intend for it to be in the future. This vision is the picture of the future that the leader must paint in enough detail for managers and workers alike to understand leadership's intended direction. If the employees of an organization are going to be asked to change, they need to know what that change will look like. And they need as much information about that change as they can get so that they can begin to integrate that picture of the future into their current way of thinking.

As we described in an earlier chapter, the vision we need to construct can either be for the entire organization undergoing change (e.g., a regional hospital becoming a cancer center) or the vision can be for one of the change projects (e.g., a tele-radiology practice to be developed in a regional hospital).

Just as a theater company needs a script to understand the new play they are to perform, organization members need a vision to understand the company the leadership wants them to be in the future. And therein lies the rub. Leaders have a tendency to state their vision for the future in terms that are too brief and too sketchy to be fully understood by the workforce ... depending on five or six bullet points on a single page to communicate what they want their organizations to become. The simple truth of the matter is that such a brief and abbreviated vision statement or slogan is totally unsatisfactory as a tool for leading organizational change.

For a vision to be useful, it must be thought through and detailed much more like the script for a play than like the bullet points we see on presentation slides. To make the point, consider this Mind-Clearing Example.

> *Mind-Clearing Example – Imagine a Director who introduces his theater company to the upcoming performance with the following description ... instead of a script. "We will be conducting a new play that people are going to rave about: it will be a musical comedy, set in contemporary New York, with songs sung by heavily-costumed cats, with great choreography! Doesn't this sound exciting?"*
>
> *Imagine the company asking for more details...and being told, "I just told you..." with an impatient repeat of the description just given.*

A vision must be constructed so that it captures the real spirit of the desired change and be detailed enough to show the future with

- Organization members (members of the radiology team) ...
- Performing new or altered work processes (providing radiation treatments as well as diagnostic services via telemedicine) ...
- Using the new or altered FET (new and more powerful x-ray equipment and telemedicine hardware/software) required by those work processes.

Required Contents for the detailed vision

At the organization level, why change? Any organizational change should count, it should be about something significant, something challenging. If not designed to make something important happen, then why bother to go to all the sweat and work of organizational change? Shouldn't we be making change happen for business reasons?

The two most important dimensions of the detailed vision are:

ROBERT CUYLER, PHD AND DUTCH HOLLAND, PHD

- **Customer/Patient Satisfaction:** organization members should be able to see well-satisfied customers or patients in the organization's vision of the future as well as the direct causes of their satisfaction.

- **Competitive advantage:** the organization members should be able to read the vision and discern the differences the change will make in order to give the organization an edge over its competitors.

If your organization begins to write its vision for the future but neither customer satisfaction nor competitive advantage are clear, then it is not time to write the vision.

Identify and dispel deadly assumptions that will disable communication of the change vision

Before we detail the steps needed to develop and test a vision for the addition of a telemedicine practice, we should examine common assumptions about vision made in most healthcare organizations. Over time organizations frequently develop assumptions that will, if used, block successful organizational change. These assumptions come into play as soon as managers begin to implement each of the five steps needed to transition an organization to a new way of doing business.

No better example of a change-blocking assumption is the one that disables communication of the vision for the transition to a new way of doing business. The table below shows one of the most deadly assumptions that impacts many if not all organizations attempting change: "people just need to be told about a new direction and they will immediately understand that direction to the level needed to move forward."

When we think about that assumption, our experience with life tells us that it is untrue; people have to hear a new message several times before they "get it." Holding such an assumption guarantees that transition will be based on minimal, single-incident under-communication. Such under-communication will likely confuse and bewilder employees and only increase anxiety about an upcoming change.

Change leaders can spot the likely presence of deadly assumptions through conversations heard about what needs to be done to communicate the vision of a new way of doing business. Hearing the suggestion to "stop all this communication planning foolishness and just tell them" calls for the change leader to surface deadly assumptions and to dispel them in any way possible, starting with the proven consequences in the table above.

Step	Deadly Assumptions	Disabling Behavior by Management	Proven Consequences
Requirement One: Communication of the Vision	People just need to be told about a new direction and they'll "get it."	• Minimal, "one-shot" communication • Token communication • Impatience in answering questions	• Rumors and miss-information • Anxiety and apprehension about change • Confusion

Take these action steps to communicate the change vision

Now we are on to the hard work of communicating the vision that will guide the organization's transition to a new way of doing business. Skip any one of the following five steps and expect expensive delays.

Action steps to communicate the change vision

- 1A: Construct the detailed vision of the future organization with telemedicine
- 1B: Construct the case for adding a telemedicine practice
- 1C: Ensure management understanding and agreement
- 1D: Communicate the vision the right way to the entire organization
- 1E: Ensure employee translation of the vision

Requirement 1A: Construct the detailed vision of the future organization containing a telemedicine practice

> ***Mind-Clearing Example** – Imagine a Director who tells the theater company, "I have it! The producer and I have decided to change to a new play that has more contemporary comedy, richer and more colorful costumes, and up-dated music. It is going to be the new rage on Broadway! I want you folks to begin thinking about your role in the new play. Isn't this exciting!"*

It is the role of the leader to ensure that there is a clear direction for any desired organizational change like the one required to onboard a telemedicine practice.

Over the years, we have seen successful changes that have started with a design that came from an autocratic decree. We have also seen changes that used a heavily participative process involving hundreds of people in the organization and its marketplace. Our favorite approach, and the one we think works best, uses a mixture of participation from those organization members who can see the future … and decisive leadership who is willing to cut off debate at some point and make a call. "Making a call" means stating for the record the direction of the desired change. An example of the desired direction of change is Bell Helicopter's vision of "having the world's most reliable helicopters and giving the world's most responsive service to its customers."

It is one thing to have the direction of organizational change in mind; it is another to give that direction a voice or a presence that organization members can grasp. In the detailing step, we want to paint a richly-textured picture of how the organization will operate after the desired change to telemedicine has been completed.

Some of the best visions we have seen for organizational change are considerably longer and more detailed than a few short bullet points on a half sheet of paper. One of our long-time clients was COO of a large financial organization. He made one pass at articulating his vision for the year 2014 for the firm's distribution system made of some 4,000 offices. His first pass was made using the traditional approach of six quick bullet points on one page. He and his direct reports conducted a half-day session with the next twenty or so managers to explain the vision … using the six bullet points as the primary explanation tool. As the session was going along, The COO leaned over to me and said, "I can tell that our message is not getting across. What do we do?"

The COO finished that session and went back to the drawing board … or in his case, the PC. Over the next week, he turned the bullet point vision into a 20+-page short story that illustrated in great detail the bullet points. His story was about a prospective employee who tried to join the financial organization in the year 2014. The COO detailed what the prospective employee did, how the organization responded, how actual people in the organization worked with the prospect … what they said and exactly what they did. After the short story was complete, the COO gave it to the same twenty or so managers who had been in the first explanation session. Their response was simple and straight forward: "Now we get it. Now we understand what the bullet points meant! And we like it!"

Test the vision for organizational change

We don't know if we have a vision statement that can guide organizational change unless we test it with organization members. We want the vision message tested to ensure that it is understandable, valid, complete, possible, compelling and able to be resourced.

One of our clients recently finished such a test with his organization. The president of this international company and some twenty members of his organization had just completed the design and detailing of their vision for the future. They wanted to gauge employee reaction to the wording of the vision before they went into organization-wide communication. About twenty employees representing both the headquarters and the field organizations were brought together for a two-hour session in which the President and his management team walked the group through the vision of the future. The President and his team found out that their vision and direction for the future were clear and compelling; but they also found out that the growth objectives in the vision were too numerous and overwhelming. Is that all, you say? Yep, it's that simple. The unfortunate fact of the matter is that many organizations launch a full-scale change effort without a simple vision test like the one recently used by our client!

Northwest Memorial Example: Constructing the detailed vision of the future organization

In this case, visions were created at two separate levels. The CMO's appointed steering committee for the System Specialty Integration Project developed the first vision as a part of their original meetings to charter the project. The comments from two or three sessions were pulled into a detailed draft of a vision for enhanced integration among the system hospitals.

That draft was later used with the leadership of each of the medical specialty sections (physicians, department heads, nurses, administrators, etc.) who "put the meat on the bones" by elaborating on the key points in the draft. In order to fully involve the physicians, the Integration agenda was placed as the first item on the schedule for each monthly medical section meeting, at the insistence of the Chief Medical Officer.

ROBERT CUYLER, PHD AND DUTCH HOLLAND, PHD

Each section physician leader was charged with the task of describing the current state of integration/collaboration with other system hospitals and identifying opportunities for improvement. After review, the Chief Medical Officer made a decision to prioritize surgery, psychiatry, and cardiology as the initial targets. Because of the distances involved among the system hospitals, the viability of telemedicine was raised as a potential means of linking the five campuses. A shared Electronic Medical Record system had been vetted and purchased and was in the process of testing and implementation in all of the system hospitals. Full functionality was expected within nine months, and was seen to be potentially helpful to telemedicine practices.

DID YOU NOTICE ?

1. Vision elements and wordings were pulled from conversations among medical leaders. That is good.
2. The CMO pulled together the draft, hopefully, using some of his/her own wording. That is also good because the CMO will be the person most likely to "talk the vision" the most, and it helps if his/her words are used.

Medi-Tel Example: Constructing the detailed vision of the future organization

The angel assembled two focus groups, one consisting of representatives of several energy and oilfield support companies and another consisting of companies that provided support services to the military, with a mix of logistical support and security companies. In these meetings, Dr. Janssen and colleagues learned that many of the participants had significant unmet medical needs that posed huge challenges and expenses. The largest of the energy companies already had well-planned and tested medical resources and was unlikely to engage with a start-up.

With these exclusions, however, the participants almost universally were challenged with the inability to access specialists that would enable them to diagnose and treat medical conditions in place or to make assessment decisions around repatriating personnel.

As might be expected, transportation costs for bringing back personnel to assess and treat medical conditions was a significant problem, but even more, companies were focused on providing the best medical care possible to their personnel. By treating personnel in place rather than airlifting out (unless medically necessary), they expected to improve health, safety, quality of life, and productivity. The participants suggested their companies would have no objection to contracting for services at premium rates given the stakes and high costs of their current systems.

The cardiologist, the managing partner of a multi-specialty group, suggested that his group had an interest in helping finance the start-up (which had been labeled Medi-Tel in early discussions) by taking an ownership stake and in providing a practice setting for the prospective participants to provide in-person medicine through the clinic as Medi-Tel grew. The arrangement ensured that each of the doctors would have an income stream during the early stages of the organization's growth.

Medi-Tel Example: Constructing the detailed vision of the future organization

The angel investor brought in his go-to attorney to recommend and draw up articles of incorporation for Medi-Tel LLC. Discussions of the various parties led to the registration of the telemedicine company, owned 30% by the multi-specialty physician practice, 10% by the angel investor, and 10% by each of the six doctor partners.

A detailed business plan was drafted and circulated among the participants, who agreed that they fund the business with $750,000 according to their pro-rata shares. Dr. Janssen would function as CEO and Chief Medical Officer, and Steven Ames, the angel investor, agreed to function as interim COO to help get the business launched. Telemedicine and Electronic Medical Record Vendors were invited in to demonstrate their product lines.

The members of the newly established Medi-Tel entity agreed to a vision of the company that emphasized the delivery of high quality medical care and consultation to companies and their personnel around the world, with a focus on providing highly-personalized *care to remote and high-risk environments via telemedicine. An advisory board was assembled that included the medical director of the multi-specialty physician group, the angel investor, a banker with healthcare background, and a local hospital CEO.*

DID YOU NOTICE

1. *A vision should describe how an organization should look and work at some future time.*
2. *A vision should be drafted after hearing first-hand from all key stakeholder groups.*
3. *An "oral idea" can be used to hold and guide stakeholder discussions. Good.*
4. *Then, finally, members of the company agreed to the vision. Bravo!*

Requirement 1B: Constructing the case for change: Why have a telemedicine practice?

Mind-Clearing Example – Imagine a Director who hands out the script for a new play without saying anything about the current play that the theatre company is performing nightly. When asked about the status of the current play, imagine the Director saying, "Oh, I don't know what we're going to do with it. Just start thinking about this new script."

Organization members seem to respond better to organizational change when they understand why the change is necessary and/or desirable. The case for organizational change is, therefore, a rational explanation of the need to change ... put in terms of value to organization members. There are several stakeholders (persons or entities that have something "at stake" with the organization) involved with every organizational change. But one stakeholder is more critical than others for the change. An organizational change must be made by the organization's members ... and they are the ones who need to see both the wisdom and the personal consequences of the change if they are to be vitally involved in making that change happen.

The case for change can be derived from another kind of future vision for the organization ... the future the organization and its employees will face if changes are not made in the way it is doing business. This method for deriving the case for change comes from a simple visioning process to predict the organization's vitality and health level if it continues to operate into the future in just the way it does now.

Develop the case for change

It is the role of the leader to ensure that there is a clear and compelling case for any desired organizational change. The method the leader uses to identify the case for change is largely immaterial. Any attempt to change an organization is a big undertaking with high stakes ... an undertaking that always has real risks to the continued healthy operation of the organization, to uninterrupted service to patients and customers, to the earnings of the investors, and to the total working compensation of the employees. If the case for change is not strong, change will be very unlikely to happen as the leader wants it to.

The case for change drives simple bottom line statements for the organization's three stakeholders. The bottom line for the case for change from the customer (patient, customer, physician, payer, etc.) point of view is simple: the case must describe a situation that the customer will find undesirable to keeping up the business relationship with the organization. The bottom line for the case for change from the investor point of view is simple: the case must describe a situation that the Board and investors will see as undesirable for themselves at a personal level. The bottom line for the case for change from the employee point of view is simple: the case must describe a situation that organization members will see as undesirable for themselves at a personal level. If a compelling case for change cannot be honestly and realistically made, the organization would be better off without it!

Test the case for organizational change

We don't know if we have a case for change that will work unless we test it with the members of the organization. We want to see if people can "identify with" the personal consequences for themselves as we unfold the case for change.

If answers from the test employees show no undesirable personal consequences, you may not have a case for change that will serve you well in the change process. If not, re-make your case or abandon your plans to make a change!

ROBERT CUYLER, PHD AND DUTCH HOLLAND, PHD

Northwest Memorial Example:
Constructing the case for change

After developing bullet point ideas for a vision of the System Specialty Integration (SSI), the Chief Medical Officer and COO of North Memorial invited five teams of stakeholders including physicians, nurses, administrators, human resources and IT professionals into individual one hour sessions to identify the pluses and minuses of the specialty targets (surgery, psychiatry, and cardiology) and the reasons why such an idea should be implemented. The teams included participation by conference lines to key individuals at the rural hospitals, although attendance and participation at the remote sites was less than optimal.

Each member of each meeting gave ideas about the reasons System Specialty Integration would be valuable for the institutions, their patients and for themselves personally. The polished notes from the meeting became the detailed description of the case for change that was used in all communication about the re-design of specialty physician services.

DID YOU NOTICE

1. Going to this level of effort to develop a case for change is just wonderful.
2. What a great approach to use the next time you lead an organizational change!

Medi-Tel Example: Constructing the case for change

The participating doctors began to grasp that they had embarked on an enterprise that would fundamentally change the way they practiced medicine. The ability to continue to see patients 'live' at the multi-specialty clinic had lulled some into believing that their practice of medicine would continue largely as usual, and that the shift to telemedicine would be gradual. Several were shocked to hear expectations from Dr. Janssen and the angel investor that they expected all of the doctors to move to a 75% telemedicine practice in the first year of operations and to expect 100% telemedicine by year two.

The financial projections for the company were aggressive and predicated on a rapid growth of clients and patient care volume. Each of the doctors would be expected to represent the company in the business development process as needed, particularly if there was a focus in their specialty area. Dr. Butler, the dermatologist, expressed discomfort with this role, seeing herself as a doctor and not a salesperson. Some of the other doctors expressed similar misgivings.

Dr. Janssen responded fairly bluntly, indicating that new roles and expectations came with the territory, and that any of the doctors who could not make needed shifts might need to reconsider whether they were making the right decision for themselves. Steve Ames, the angel investor, offered himself as a mentor, having worked with a number of physicians in previous start-ups. He agreed also that he would be involved in each of the customer contacts in the early stages to get the doctors comfortable in the sales process. He emphasized that their clinical reputations and skill sets were the key ingredients of their contribution.

DID YOU NOTICE

1. Doctors were told about the change and thought they understood. Good start.
2. Real understanding of change comes only with experiencing the actual change. This is OK. Just be prepared if you are the change leader.
3. Complaints from the docs would have been the ideal excuse to change the plan, to compromise the design ... and to compromise the business. Bravo, Dr. Janssen!
4. Some physicians did not see themselves as business developers or as "salespersons." Advice to the docs? "Get over it! Welcome to 21st century medicine!"

ROBERT CUYLER, PHD AND DUTCH HOLLAND, PHD

Requirement 1C: Ensure management understanding of and commitment to the vision of telemedicine

> *Mind-Clearing Example – Imagine a Director who is communicating the new play to the bit actors and stage hands while the lead actors and the stage manager look on ... and shake their heads in disagreement with everything the Director says.*
>
> *Imagine the musicians hearing the Director with one ear while hearing the conductor mumble to those around him, "Really dumb idea! This score is going to be a joke!"*

Organization members react to their bosses. Period. If you want to make an organizational change, you better get all the managers in the organization signed up and ready to play ... or the change is not likely to work. It is critical for all managers to

- Understand the vision and case for organizational change,
- Understand leadership's expectations that all managers be a part of leading/managing the change,
- Be totally committed to making the change happen.

Many leaders would think that this is a tall order ... and it may be in some organizations. But our advice is simple, do not attempt a change without the managers on board. If the change is required for business success, you can either get all your mangers on board ... or change to managers who will be on board!

We have seen more change efforts scuttled by uncommitted managers than by any other problem. Managers who are not committed to the change are a clear mixed signal to employees. If top management signals a change but other managers don't go along with it, the employees are in a box ... and they will usually resolve their mixed feelings by taking the position of the manager who is closest to them on the organization chart. All organization members are responsible to somebody in the organizational hierarchy ... that's what we figure out after only a few days on the job. It is totally nonsensical to ask an organization member to put her job in jeopardy by taking up a change that her boss doesn't agree with!

It has always struck us as very interesting that organizations go through tough exercises to face the reality of their marketplace and decide that they must change … and then serve up that change to the organization as though the change were optional! We don't mean that managers stand in front of employees and use the word "optional" with regard to change … they don't. But they do talk about the change in such "iffy" and participative tones that employee wind up feeling the change is optional. Sometimes managers go out of their way to be sensitive to employee feelings, and ask employees about the change rather than announcing that the change will occur.

If the organization needs to change for prosperity or survival sake, then the change is not optional! Announce the change, don't ask the organization what they want to do. If the change is required for organizational prosperity or survival reasons, there is no way out … the organization must change. Organization members always have the option of going along with the change or not … translated to mean "staying in the organization and cooperating in the change or leaving the organization."

When we receive harsh criticism about our "change is not an option" message, we ask, "Should the director of a new play allow key actors to stay in the cast and act a different play on stage while the rest of the theater company performs the new play on the same stage?"

Conducting management work-through sessions

We have found that getting management on board for a change is much easier if what we call work-through sessions are conducted with all managers who have a part or stake in the change. The purpose of the sessions is to allow managers to (1) absorb the idea of the change and the resulting organization structure and to (2) work through the ramifications of the change for themselves and their troops. The sessions are also the opportunity to get management "in the know" before their employees get introduced to the change. Managers must be in the know first … lest their authority and credibility be undercut with their employees … who need to know and feel that their boss is part of the leadership structure of the company.

Management work-through sessions are simply meetings of groups of mangers with the leaders of the company to discuss the impending change. The key idea is to allow the mangers the opportunity to hear about the impending change first hand, to ask questions about the change, and even to challenge the change ... both from a rational and technical point of view. After all, we pay managers to question and challenge ideas to ensure their validity before action. So why not allow that challenge here? In many such sessions we have seen big issues resolve and great ideas be developed that add to the design of the vision and the case for change.

We have also seen the effect of different learning styles in such discussions. With certain adult learners, the need to question and criticize something, to state "that will never work" and so forth, is necessary for hearing and understanding. The leader's role is to keep his cool during the discussions and trust that most managers will both understand the impending change, and recognize that their job is to make that change happen.

Now before we get into the detailed methods for a work-through session, let's remember where we are in the organizational change. We have already developed and tested our vision for organizational change and the case for change. Several of the managers we are about to address may have already been involved in developing either the vision or the case for change. In either case, the change has been decided, and there is no turning back.

During the conduct of the work-through sessions, it is critical for the leader to lead the change in word and deed. We mean the following:

1. **Change for the better:** The leader should convey her excitement about the opportunity to change the organization for the better and her confidence that the change will be good for the organization.

2. **Change will be worth it:** The leader should acknowledge the difficulty that comes with organizational change and clearly state his conviction that the organization and employees will be in a better place after the change has been completed.

3. **Change is not an option:** The leader should clearly convey that the change is not an option at this point. Senior management has considered the options and picked this one! The challenge is to implement that change.

4. **The job is to change:** The leader should have a presence and tone that says, "We are making this change happen because it is our job. I am in control of the change, and it will happen on time, on target, and on budget." The leader, like an actor, must look serious and committed to the change.

5. **All Managers make change happen:** The leader should clearly convey her expectation that all the mangers in the firm will be on board and help with the implementation of the change.

6. **Management teamwork for change:** The leader should convey the message that the change will be done in an orderly planned way with each member of the management team doing his/her part to make the change happen.

We cannot over-emphasize the importance of leadership presence during this critical step in change. These manager work-through sessions are critical for the organizational change … and the leader must look and be positive, serious and committed or the sessions will move the change backward and not forward!

Testing management to ensure they are on board

Management work-through is not complete until we have ensured that all of our managers are on board with the change. The only way to ensure understanding of the impending change and willingness to be a part of leading the organization through it is to conduct a face-to-face meeting, one-on-one with each manager in the organization. In that meeting the leader hears and sees for herself that the manager does understand both the vision and the case for change. The manager might ask questions such as:

- What do you think the most important part of the change will be for your unit?
- How do you plan to explain the case for change to your team?

The bottom line is that the questions are not important. What is important is that the leader interact long enough with the manager around the change to reassure herself that the manager has understood the vision and case for change.

After ensuring understanding, the leader must move on to reassure herself that the manager is willing to support the change. (Remember that we said the change is not optional for the organization. That doesn't mean that all organization members will be willing to go along with it). The best way to deal with the "readiness to support" issue is simply to ask the manager point blank: "Can I count on you? Are you ready to support me to make this change happen on target, on time, and on budget?" Since many employees would be reluctant to give any answer other than "yes," the leader should hold out an honest offer to allow the manager to consider the questions and come see the leader before the week is over. The leader should say, "Please see me personally before the end of the week to give me your answer."

> Now get this, the leader closes the one-on-one meeting with the manager with our cultural signal of business agreement... the handshake. This handshake clearly symbolizes a business agreement and is the single most compelling action the leader can take with a manager. The handshake means that the manager understands the impending change and the leader's expectation that the manager will be involved in implementing it.

For organizations with more than one level of management between the leader and the employees, management work through sessions will need to be conducted a layer of management at a time until the entire chain of command has been brought to a common level of understanding and willingness to implement. That is, we do not want to put several layers of management in the same room at the same time for work-through sessions for a key reason. We want to maintain the authority of the chain of command and the credibility of each manager by having her work through the change message before her direct reports do. We want her to feel free to question and even argue about the upcoming change and get on board with it before she works the change with her direct reports. If a manager and her direct reports hear about a change at the same time, the direct reports will wonder why their boss wasn't in on or privy to the leadership decision about change.

Northwest Memorial Example:
Conducting management work-through sessions

Expertise in telemedicine was limited within the system, so a recommendation was made to create a position of System Telemedicine Coordinator, reporting to the System IT Director. The Chief Strategy Officer (CSO) learned an important lesson when realizing that the Telemedicine Coordinator did not have the real or perceived power within the organization, particularly the rural affiliates, to quarterback a significant change initiative.

New to the organization, the Telemedicine Coordinator was not aware of the larger problems of system integration that were at play. While most of the stakeholders were on board with the telemedicine project 'in concept,' it was clear that few had anticipated all of the moving parts involved or the personal and organizational commitment that would be involved. Additionally, there was no established pathway for clinical collaboration among the System hospitals. While some progress was being made in areas such as group purchasing, the five hospitals at the service level continued to function as independent entities.

The Chief Strategy Officer enlisted the System CEO to highlight the Telemedicine project at the next System Executives gathering, which would bring together the 'C-Suites' of all the member hospitals. The CEO and CSO summarized the history of integration challenges within the system and invited the participants to identify the major changes involved in the Telemedicine project and the factors that could hinder implementation.

Frank discussion of revenue and expense emerged, as the rural hospital leadership clearly had some concerns that they would incur additional equipment and staff expenses while revenues would primarily flow to the urban hub. The Chief Strategy Officer acknowledged the concerns but stressed the challenges of out-migration of surgeries and the presence of the primary care practices of the competing system in their

ROBERT CUYLER, PHD AND DUTCH HOLLAND, PHD

service areas. The CEO then stressed that the System could not afford to stand by as competitors exercised their playbooks. Further, the System had innovative approaches to improve collaboration, community health, and the bottom line by linking their resources.

The CEO asked for the commitment of all of the administrative teams and pointed out that this would be first of many initiatives that would challenge the old way of doing business.

DID YOU NOTICE

1. Staff does not explain organizational change. Executives do.
2. Management work-through sessions should solicit issues and problems to be discussed. That is why the sessions are called "work through!"
3. Use the CEO in organizational change. That is why there is a Chief Executive Officer in the first place!
4. The CEO points out competitive advantage as the goal. Why change if you are not focused on gaining competitive advantage? Bravo!

Requirement 1D: Communicating the telemedicine vision the right way

> *Mind-Clearing Example – Imagine a Director who is trying to communicate the new play to a theater company with an opener like this, "OK folks, I'm only going to tell you the contents of this play one time…"*
>
> *Or imagine that Director giving out only one copy of the script for the entire theater company. Better yet, imagine the Director who says, "I don't want to bore you with all the details of the script, so here is a memo summarizing the key themes in the play."*

Communicating the vision and case for organization change the right way is a simple idea that is tough to execute. The right way means to communicate the message so that every member of the organization that is changing gets to hear the message enough times and in enough ways to be able to understand what they need to do. Our experience is that most leaders start the communication process with good intentions, but they typically do not follow through with the detailed steps that are needed. Successful organizational change depends on a systematic approach to communicating change.

Plan for communicating change

Communicating a new play to a theater company of two dozen can be a relatively simple exercise of calling one all-hands meeting and talking everyone through the script, encouraging them to take notes in their individual copies of the script and to ask questions until they felt comfortable. But for an organization of 14,000 employees spread over 30 countries, communication is not quite so easy.

For a change situation like this, a comprehensive communication plan is needed. The plan must identify the specific populations among the employees, the specific location of those employees, their work shifts/schedules, the languages and/or cultures, the communication devices that are available, and the overall timetable for the impending change. The bottom line requirement for the communication plan is that it be a detailed solution to the problem of getting each person the information he needs, when he needs it, to have him be involved in a change that occurs on target, on time, and on budget.

Use all available communication devices

Most companies already have a variety of communication devices that they use in their day-to-day businesses. The primary decision communication device in an organization is the chain of command ... the direct linkages between a boss and every member of the organization. This primary channel must be used to communicate about organizational change or the members of the organization will not see information about impending change as having anything important to do with them. Other communication devices, like electronic bulletin boards, newsletters, training classes, safety meetings, and staff meetings are already standard and accepted means of communication. These other devices should be used to accompany and/or reinforce the chain of command message ... but they can never substitute for it!

We know that it is not popular in some circles to even mention a phrase from the past ... like "chain of command" ... but the truth is, every organization has one, and the employees in every organization respond to it. This chain

ROBERT CUYLER, PHD AND DUTCH HOLLAND, PHD

of command linkage between boss and organization member is a primary mechanical connection that makes up a part of the structure of any organization. Organizations cannot be changed on target, on time and on budget without using the chain of command linkage. Imagine a theater company without a Director trying to get a new play ready and onto the stage.

Use proven communication principles

There are four principles that we believe are required for effective communication about impending organizational change. (See the appendix for more details on principles)

1. **Two-way communication** – that allows organization members to ask questions and give feedback about the change – is required for a high comprehension level.

2. **All communication bases** should be used including visual, aural and emotional messages.

3. **Repetition** will be required to convey a change message to the entire organization.

4. **Rich, face-to-face communication** will be required for organization members to communicate at maximum levels of effectiveness about the change.

Work the communication plan to desired results

Plan your work and work your plan. In the context of communicating change, working your plan is important … and working your plan well, crisply, and in a well-organized way can take you a long way toward successful organizational change. We have seen great damage done to change efforts by managers who are unprepared to communicate change. We can hardly expect an organization to change on target, on time and on budget if the organization's managers cannot even communicate about the impending change on target, on time, and on budget! Imagine what it says to an organization when its managers start the change communication meeting late, without needed materials, with unfocused projectors, poorly prepared slides, and unrehearsed remarks!

Leaders have not mastered change until they can communicate about organizational change with the same effectiveness and efficiency they have in the way they communicate routine changes in production runs, part numbers, sales prices, policies, priorities, or accreditation requirements.

Northwest Memorial Example: Communicating the Vision the Right Way

With the help of two internal communication specialists, the SSI narrative took shape. The plan called for written version of the vision, clever posters for walls, a special newsletter mailed to every employee, and a website that described the SSI offerings. In addition, the quarterly grand rounds meetings for a full year were devoted to continue to communicate about SSI as well as about progress being made in its implementation.

DID YOU NOTICE

1. Posters are handy, and newsletters are dandy, but don't stop.
2. Communication at Grand Rounds on a continual basis gives the change the gravitas it needs to be seen as a real priority. Bravo!
3. Physicians don't come to Grand Rounds? An important communication linkage is broken. Time for a change.

Northwest Memorial Example: Complications in Communicating the Vision

The System's Telemedicine Coordinator, new to the organization and reporting to the Director of Information Technology, found it difficult to schedule appointments and get emails answered with a number of key stakeholders in Memorial's SSI project. Tasked with developing a communication plan that would describe and disseminate Memorial's plans to use telemedicine to spread specialty care, the Telemedicine Coordinator struggled to make deadlines and produce compelling written materials. Initially frustrated with the lack of progress, the COO soon realized that the Telemedicine Coordinator was being tasked with formulating an initiative which was of key strategic importance to the organization. She further realized

ROBERT CUYLER, PHD AND DUTCH HOLLAND, PHD

that the SSI program had much more to do with workflow and inter-hospital relationships than with technology.

Leadership of the SSI program was re-assigned to the System's Chief Strategy Officer, and the Telemedicine Coordinator's position was re-designed to report to the CSO. With the organizational visibility and influence to drive communication and collaboration, the CSO chaired subsequent meetings and took a lead role in articulating the System's SSI strategy, assisted by the Telemedicine Coordinator.

DID YOU NOTICE

1. Should we have to wait to "figure something out by trial and error?"
2. Read a book, buy a methodology, or hire a fishing guide. Anything beats crushing an innocent staffer in a job he has no rank or authority to do.

Medi-Tel Example: Communicating the Vision the Right Way

Steve Ames enlisted the marketing/community relations director of the medical practice to draft a formal version of a vision statement and to interview each of the telemedicine doctors to identify key features of experience and background, as the doctors would be featured quite extensively to capitalize on their expertise and to 'give a face' to the enterprise. Ames called on one of the oilfield service company owners he knew well to 'field trial' the initial drafts of the vision statement and marketing materials to insure that these were tuned into potential customer needs.

The Medi-Tel group met with the Advisory Board to present the vision statement and goals of the company. The Advisory Board members had many suggestions for potential customers as well as advising about the many potential stumbling blocks that new businesses can face. They offered consultation as needed to Medi-Tel to assist with the company's formation, launch, and growth.

1. Communication the right way.
2. Textbook. Bravo!

Requirement 1E: Ensure employee personal translation of the telemedicine vision

> *Mind-Clearing Example – Imagine a Director who is handing out scripts for the new play. When an actor asks, "Who am I in the new play?" the Director simply responds, "Oh, I don't know. Just read the whole thing, and we'll work all that out later." Or worse yet, imagine the Director saying, "I haven't even thought about you in the context of the new play. But just give it a read anyway."*

Organization members are not ready to begin an organizational change until they can personally relate to it. The purpose of Personal Application Sessions is to bring all employees affected by the impending change to a level of comprehension and to ensure that they are on board for the change. Personal Application Sessions are very similar to the manager work-through sessions we described earlier.

Every manager whose department or unit is affected by the change must conduct Personal Application Sessions with her workers. The process includes a meeting of all employees reporting to that manager followed by a face-to-face, one-on-one session between manager and each employee.

During the conduct of the personal application sessions, the manager must lead the change with the same serious and committed tone and attitude we identified earlier for the leaders of management work-through sessions.

Northwest Memorial Example:
Ensure Employee Translation of the Vision

Each manager in the central Northwest Memorial campus was asked by the Telemedicine Coordinator to hold one-on-one sessions with the surgery, cardiology, and psychiatry physicians and their nurse managers involved in the Telemedicine project and to report back on the results of the conversations by a named date. The Telemedicine Coordinator made visits in person to each of the four rural hospitals to meet with Administration and directors/nurse managers of Surgery, Emergency Department, and Outpatient Clinic.

The sessions brought out the fact that the psychiatrists were interested in assisting in the Telemedicine project but were concerned about the potential frequency of Emergency Department consultation requests. The psychiatrists were reminded that the Mobile Crisis Team would continue to take the large majority of the calls and would also be able to respond by videoconference to the outlying Emergency Departments. One of the psychiatrists, who could be considered an 'Early Adopter' offered to train the Mobile Crisis Team on determining which patients would need a physician examination and to develop a protocol for defining the reason for referral to a psychiatrist. The Psychiatry Section Chief determined that the budget allowed for 'On Call' payments to psychiatrists for evening and weekend coverage and that staffing would allow for call duty one week out of six.

The cardiologists at Northwest Memorial were adamant that first patient visits be conducted 'face to face' in order to establish a strong doctor-patient relationship and to allow for some diagnostic tests not available at all of the rural affiliates. The Chief Strategy Officer accepted the protocol but asked for review three and six months after implementation to re-assess the cardiologists comfort level with Telemedicine and to determine if more of the consultations could be accomplished via telemedicine after a pilot period.

The surgical nurse managers at the rural hospitals pointed out that they would need to balance their staffing levels and duties for cases performed at their hospitals with the need to 'tele-present' patients for pre- and post-procedure consults. One nurse manager reported that each hospital's PRN pool had nursing candidates with OR experience who could be trained to tele-present and were interested in picking up paid hours.

1. Talking over the change with the troops is critical.
2. Talking over the change on a one-on-one basis allows each player to understand and get in or get out.
3. One-on-one's are a required start to the organizational change process, and are likely to generate both enthusiasm and ideas.

And in conclusion ...

Just as a theater company needs a script to understand the new play they are to perform, organization members need a vision to understand the company the leadership wants them to be in the future. Requirement One calls for leaders to construct and fully communicate a clear, detailed vision of the organization as they intend for it to be in the future. If the employees of an organization are going to be asked to change, they need to know what that change will look like. And they need as much information about that change as they can get so that they can begin to integrate that picture of the future into their way of thinking.

The vision we need to construct can either be for the entire organization undergoing change (e.g., a regional hospital becoming a cancer center) or the vision can be for one of the change projects (e.g., a tele-radiology practice to be developed in the hospital).

A vision for change is certainly critical. A vision is necessary, but not sufficient for change. A vision, regardless of how well communicated is not enough to lead a successful organizational change. The other moving parts of an organization described in later chapters will tell the rest of the story. When taken together, vision and the other moving parts will be sufficient for an organizational change ... on target, on time, and on budget.

ROBERT CUYLER, PHD AND DUTCH HOLLAND, PHD

CHAPTER THREE

Alter Work Processes and Procedures for Telemedicine

Mind-Clearing Example – Imagine a Director who assumes that everything that needs to be worked out about the actors' performance is in the script. "It is all written right there ... and you can probably do some stuff that was in the last play!"

Imagine not working out detailed game plans for starting and stopping the music, when curtains are to open and close, when scenery and backdrops are to be changed, when actors enter and leave the stage, etc. etc.

IMPLEMENTATION OF THE telemedicine vision cannot occur until existing processes and procedures are physically modified to enable a new way of doing business. Implementation cannot occur until the machinery of the workflow is successfully altered and tested. In this chapter we will focus on changing the physical steps the organization will need to use in the new way of doing business. Failing to alter work processes and still expecting operation of a telemedicine practice is akin to expecting the performance of a new play from a theater company that is still operating with the old script.

Identify and dispel deadly assumptions that will disable transition to the telemedicine vision

The step of altering work processes to enable the change vision is perhaps the most important to "get right." Process steps make something out of nothing, and without processes there would be no organizational outcomes. When transitioning an organization to a new way of doing business, very careful attention must be paid to the validity of the process steps that will make up the new way of doing business.

However, in the day-to-day running of a business, many process steps are practically invisible as employees complete work steps that they have been completing for some time. In many cases, employees are blind to the reasons or thinking behind the steps they currently complete, not having had to develop those steps through design or trial and error. The tendency of many managers is, therefore, to assume that "people know the process steps" and if changes are needed, employees will work them out as they go along toward the new way of doing business. But such is not the case as many who have left processes to meander toward the future have found out.

Step	Change-Blocking Assumption	Disabling Behavior of Management	Proven Consequences
Requirement Two: Alteration of Process(es) and Procedures	If people understand the direction of change, they will start using the correct processes and procedures automatically.	Managers downplaying process analysis; depending on individuals to work through processes and procedures themselves.	• Inconsistent performance • Sub-optimized improvement • Anxiety • Botched procedures

Change leaders can spot the likely presence of deadly assumptions about work processes through conversations heard about what needs to be done. Hearing the suggestion "We don't need all this process mapping stuff; our people will shift to new processes automatically as we go along" calls for the change leader to surface deadly assumptions and to dispel them in any way possible, starting with the proven consequences in the table above.

Take these action steps to alter work processes for telemedicine

Now we are on to the hard work of transitioning work processes using the following five steps. Skip a step and expect expensive delays.

Action steps to transition work processes

- 2A: Identify work process alternations needed for telemedicine
- 2B: Alter and test work processes critical for the implementation of telemedicine
- 2C: Alter process measures, goals, and objectives to match processes

ROBERT CUYLER, PHD AND DUTCH HOLLAND, PHD

- 2D: Alter and test work procedures for altered work processes
- 2E: Eliminate old measures, goals, objectives and procedures

Requirement 2A: Identify the process alterations needed for telemedicine

> *Mind-Clearing Example – Imagine a Director who has not worked through in her mind exactly what she wants the actors to do in their newly assigned roles.*
>
> *Imagine she knows that she wants to depict young men in the streets committed to revolution but she has not yet visualized or communicated the "manning of the barricades" on stage. Or imagine the Director who transitions the company to a new play but who allows the actors to repeat the scenes from the previous play!*

If a theater company doesn't change what happens on stage, the audience will swear that the play has not changed ... despite the new name on the marquee. If the day-in and day-out steps organization members take as they go about their work do not change, then the organization has not changed ... despite any words, slogans, or banners to the contrary.

We can imagine a reader inexperienced in the street-fighting of organizational change wondering why we are making such "no brainer" assertions. After watching organizational change for thirty years, we will tell you that it is common place for organizations to come up with a statement of new direction or plan, a new vision, and still conduct day-to-day operations in essentially the same way ... leaving the optimists among the workforce to wait for a miracle and the cynical to wait for the change effort to crater or be allowed to slowly fade away.

Changing the way the organization does business requires work process alterations

By virtue of the mechanical nature of organizations, every organizational change (like implementing telemedicine) requires at least one change in work process. Regardless of the kind of organizational change or the stimulus for organizational change, work process alterations will be required.

- If an organization decides to change its business strategy (e.g., to become the low cost service provider), many, if not all, of the organization's service delivery processes will need to change to take out costly non-value adding steps or to alter the sequence of those steps. In addition, the organization's marketing process would need to be altered to add the steps and promotional materials that stress changed features that make it better than the competition.

- If an organization decides to install Pyxis machines to expedite drug administration, work process changes will be involved. Work steps will need to change in order to set-up the new equipment. New software interfaces, for instance, will be required to communicate with the hospital's information system, and so on.

- If an organization decides to make a change in its culture (e.g., defined as "the way we do things around here"), several process changes will need to be made to require organization members to approach their jobs differently. If for example, the desired cultural change is to become more attentive to customers, changes will probably need to be made in the steps and mindsets used in the customer service delivery system including decreasing response time, informing customers what to expect, expressing concern, etc.

Start with an Inventory of Work Processes

The first step in identifying needed work process alterations is to systematically review the organization's work processes and visualize any alterations that will be needed, given the vision of implementing a telemedicine practice. We have found it easier to identify work processes that will be affected by an impending change by looking through the organization's existing inventory of work processes.

In case the organization does not have a work process inventory – and many organizations do not – we have found the following list of generic processes to be a good stimulant for discussion as organization members look for processes that might need to be altered.

While the names that organizations use for their own work processes vary greatly, almost all organizations need to use the following direct work processes in order to stay in business:

ROBERT CUYLER, PHD AND DUTCH HOLLAND, PHD

- Identify groups of customers to whom the organization's services might be provided
- Develop services that can be competitively negotiated and delivered in those markets
- Get contracts for the organization's services with third party payers within those markets
- Provide services (quality, satisfaction, outcomes) that fulfill the customers' needs
- Provide support to customers after service delivery
- Bill customers/payers for services rendered ... and receive payments

Obviously there are many sub-processes that make up each of these direct processes. For example, under the "get contracts (make sales)" work process, there will be sub-processes to identify prospects, research needs of those prospects, schedule negotiation calls, conduct marketing engagements, etc.

In searching for processes that might need to be altered, be aware that such a process could be almost anywhere in the organization. In addition to the direct work processes cited above, organizations also have processes that manage the performance of the business as a whole (executive decision-making processes), business processes (annual budgeting), and employees processes (performance appraisal systems). Hospitals also have processes with broad sweeping titles such as: human resources, information technology, finance and administration, corporate communication and public relations as well as service delivery work processes such as admitting, discharging, bed control, transferring, consult services, strategic planning, and so on. Yes, it can be like an Easter egg hunt to find and target processes. Someone also said that it was a bit like shooting pool ... since altering one process might require altering another and another and so on.

There is nothing elegant about the process inventory work described above. Inventorying is a comprehensive mechanical exercise designed to be thorough ... not elegant. While some organization members describe the process of identifying needed alterations as fun, others see it as pure drudgery. Regardless of the attitude, fun or not fun, this step must be done and done well. Many changes have gone awry because the change planners did not take the time to comprehensively review all of their organization's work processes and specifically identify the alteration work needed for the change to a new way of doing business.

Northwest Memorial Example: Identify the Process Alterations Needed for Change

Each of the clinical departments recognized that access to medical records in electronic format was critical for giving the consulting physicians access to patient records needed to deliver a sound telemedicine encounter. Because of the EMR system being installed, labs and imaging generated at the time of the consultation would be soon accessible to physicians regardless of location.

However, in the interim, paper medical records for contemporary as well as past care would have to be delivered to the consulting physicians. The IT Director and a technical representative from the EMR vendor were tasked to find an interim solution for transmitting medical records to the urban specialists and to carefully examine the document management features of the impending EMR to make sure that processes for remote log-in, physician order entry, and document exchange were thoroughly examined for telemedicine applications.

Until the EMR was fully functional, scheduling would have to be accomplished by secure email or phone. Upon review, the physicians involved preferred to have requests for consultation called into the physician offices, as they were keen to remain in charge of their schedules in the usual manner. Emergency Calls for psychiatry would be placed by the Mobile Crisis Team, whose personnel maintain a call schedule and physician contact numbers.

DID YOU NOTICE

1. The devil really is in the details, the work process details, that is.
2. Failure to get into the details or glossing over the details has been the ruin of many an organizational change and implementation.
3. Northwest Memorial worked the details! Bravo!

ROBERT CUYLER, PHD AND DUTCH HOLLAND, PHD

Medi-Tel Example: Identify the Process Alterations Needed for Change

Dr. Janssen was the only doctor among his colleagues who had practiced telemedicine. The group equipped two clinical studios with demo videoconference camera and telemedicine peripherals to give the doctors hands-on experience with the cameras and medical devices. With this structure, the doctors were able to acquaint themselves with the equipment while practicing on one another with examination scopes, peripheral cameras, and stethoscopes. Dr. Janssen educated on some of the fine points involved in examining a patient remotely and the training required at the patient side for a nurse to use the peripheral devices and to communicate effectively with the doctor.

The physicians also began to grasp the complexity of documenting care to a variety of client settings, some medical and some civilian, some with their own EMR and some with nothing. Realizing this, the group recognized that they would need to look more deeply into the workflow involved in delivering telemedicine and that much more detailed discussions were needed with potential EMR vendors to make sure they were purchasing a system that would meet their complex needs.

The infrastructure necessary to triage and schedule requests for medical consultation from many distant client locations seemed equally daunting. Because of time zone differences and the intent to offer emergency services, Medi-Tel would need a call center and trained personnel to take requests from clients and route them to the right physician, based on specialty and availability. While the call resources of the parent clinic may suffice in the beginning, the personnel involved would need to be trained and managed for the new endeavor, with some real concern that the needs of this start-up would be layered on top of existing job responsibilities. Customers' calls for services would be the initial interface. Mistakes in this transaction could gravely damage the early operations and reputation of Medi-Tel.

Dr. Janssen called on the Medical Director of the multi-specialty group to clarify the level of support that Medi-Tel could depend on from the medical group for a number of key functions such as scheduling. The Medical Director reiterated his support for Medi-Tel but cautioned Dr. Janssen to budget for staff increases as Medi-Tel grew, as the needs of the new company could not take precedence over their core job

DID YOU NOTICE

1. There is no substitute for telemedicine business experience. Don't leave home without it.
2. More discussion with the vendors are nice and frequently informative.
3. However, in the world of IT vendors, discussions will never make sure of anything!
4. Seeing and then seeing again is believing. Nothing else.
5. Clarifying the level of support (and then shaking hands on it) is not just a good idea but a requirement!
6. In the heat of battle in an organizational change, they are planning beyond the change into the future (i.e., the next change)! Bravo!

Requirement 2B: Alter and test work processes critical for the implementation of telemedicine

Mind-Clearing Example – Imagine a Director who has an idea about what an actor in the new play should be doing, but who fails to work through the details of the idea with the actor.

Or imagine the Director working through the new ideas in his mind but not actually testing them with the actors on stage. When asked specifically by an actor what he should do, the Director responded, "Oh, don't worry, we will work that through on Opening Night!"

The tendency in organizational change is to talk about how the organization needs to do business differently but to not really do anything about it. That same tendency is alive and well in the area of work process alteration. The steps in the work processes that have been identified for alteration must be physically altered, not just discussed. But where does this alteration take place? It takes place first and foremost on paper (or on a software program) and second in the trenches where the organization's workers actually use the new process steps as a part of the new way of doing day-to-day work.

Draw pictures of new work processes

The key step in physically altering work processes is to draw a picture or a "workflow diagram," much like an architect would do, of the new steps required for each work process to be altered. Most organizations today already have experience with process mapping and documentation. And many organizations are already using automated tools for such mapping ... so use them! Our purpose in this book is not to describe the well-developed fields of process improvement or process mapping. Our purpose is to make the point that many of the tools of process improvement, especially process mapping, should be applied in every organizational change!

We have had clients push back when we tell them that mapping process alterations is a must. Several have responded, "I thought we did all that during our emphasis on Total Quality Management!" Our response is simple. We must re-map processes as a part of every organizational change ... or there will be no organizational change. Altering processes remains a requirement ... despite how detailed and tedious it might be and despite how much work has been done on work processes in the past. Imagine the theater Director who makes the following bizarre statement, "No need to think through the details of roles in the new play, and writing them down will be a waste of time; we did detailed thinking for roles in the previous play!"

Northwest Memorial Example: Alter and test work processes critical to the change

Discussion with the System IT Director and an EMR vendor representative proposed a solution for handling paper documents until the EMR was fully functional. With decades of paper documents in archive, the team realized that managing paper would continue to be necessary even when the new EMR was in place, so that old records could be digitized and loaded as necessary into active charts. A $500 high-speed scanner was located which could upload records into the existing *physician electronic portal. A responsible staff member at each rural hospital would be trained to register patients for their telemedicine consultation and to upload requested documents by 3pm on the day prior to the consultation.*

DID YOU NOTICE

1. *Do not pin your hopes on an IT system.*
2. *Make it work anyway you can and then let the IT system catch up if it can.*

Medi-Tel Example: Alter and test work processes critical to the change

Dr. Eaton, the cardiologist, demoed four digital stethoscopes to review sound quality and ergonomics. As the stethoscope would not be in the hands of the telemedicine physician, a nurse or equivalent at the patient side would be placing the device. Dr. Eaton soon realized that in addition to choice of device, she would need to establish protocols to train the tele-presenter to properly position the device on the patient to insure quality. She began to jot notes to establish what a typical examination pattern would look like and to sketch the hand signals she might use to cue the tele-presenter to specify where the scope would be placed to hear heart and lung sounds.

Dr. Butler, the dermatologist, seemed absorbed in day-to-day practice and did a more cursory review of the telemedicine cameras. He was quite confident that he could use readily available technologies and adapt his practice as necessary when the time came. When his review of the equipment choices was much less detailed and in depth than that of the other specialists, Dr. Janssen became alarmed and took Dr. Butler aside for a discussion. Dr. Janssen pointed out that the shift to a telemedicine practice in dermatology was major and would involve both the 'live' examination of patients as well as reviewing 'store and forward' images.

Dr. Janssen further pointed out that dermatology to the remote sites would involve much more emergency medicine for trauma such

ROBERT CUYLER, PHD AND DUTCH HOLLAND, PHD

as burns as well as interfacing with infectious disease for clients in tropical and developing world locations. Dr. Janssen left cautiously optimistic that his colleague would make the necessary shifts but also realized that Dr. Butler was potentially a poor fit for the new enterprise.

Since none of the doctors could be expected to provide 24/7 availability, each was directed to make initial approaches to trusted colleagues in their specialty to join a contract pool that would assist with rotating call.

DID YOU NOTICE

1. A good change leader fixes problems as quickly as possible after the problem arises.
2. A great change leader begins to work a potential problem as soon as he senses it! Bravo, Dr. Janssen!

Requirement 2C: Alter work process measures, goals and objectives

> *Mind-Clearing Example – Imagine an actor in a comedy role being transferred to the role of the "serious villain" in a new play. Imagine the Director now saying to the actor, "Remember, your objective on the stage is to make the audience laugh." When questioned by the actor, the Director responds by saying, "Yes, we are changing the play, but we're not changing any goals at the individual actor level."*

We said earlier that a work process alteration would be involved in some way or another in every organizational change. There may be times when the work process steps may not need to be altered ... if the measures, goals and objectives of the work processes are altered. We can illustrate that idea with a simple example. Imagine a marketing work process for a company that sells telephone systems to medical practices. Assume that the following steps were being used for identification of prospects in a geographical market:

- Locate Chamber of Commerce directory for target market
- Review listings in the directory to identify all multi-physician practices

- Transfer practice address/phone number and names of key physicians to prospect list
- Assign market reps to call listed names to find out information about phone needs

Now let's assume that this company wants to change its strategy to include individual physician practices. All the work steps would remain essentially the same. No new process maps would need to be drawn.

Northwest Memorial Example:
Alter Process Measures, Goals and Objectives

The Telemedicine project team worked to develop tracking mechanisms that would enable the System to evaluate the impact of the three service groups using telemedicine. At each of the participating rural hospitals, the following data would be tracked:

A) *Surgery: The type and number of surgeries performed at Northwest Memorial originating from the service areas of each rural hospital will be tracked on a spreadsheet, with additional tracking of the presence of pre-op and post-op telemedicine consultation. The surgical volumes will be trended to measure whether cases were remaining within the System, reversing the out-migration patterns. Patient satisfaction data will be reviewed by the Telemedicine work group to determine if the availability of pre- and post-op telemedicine consults is affecting patient satisfaction.*

B) *Psychiatry: Volume and type of psychiatric consultation in the rural hospital ED's will be tracked. Trend data one year prior to availability of tele-psychiatry will be reviewed to establish a benchmark. ED length of stay and sitter/transportation costs will be compared for pre- and post-project time frames.*

C) *Cardiology: Volumes, patient satisfaction, and cancellation/no-show rates will be tracked for patients referred for tele-cardiology management by medical staff of the four rural hospitals.*

ROBERT CUYLER, PHD AND DUTCH HOLLAND, PHD

DID YOU NOTICE

1. If you can't measure it, you can't manage it. If you cannot say it, you cannot lead it. So goes the saying that applies here.
2. Just remember that somebody in or near your organization loves "data." Find that person and harness him or her before you start change operations or you will never catch up.

Medi-Tel Example:
Alter Process Measures, Goals and Objectives

The practice management and billing software was modified to include a telemedicine code to be attached to any physician billing. In this way, Medi-Tel could closely follow volumes and revenues associated with the growth of telemedicine cases. As the physicians were expected to be involved in a variety of activities related to the start up, productivity measures related to income and bonuses were revised. Individual bonuses linked to patient care revenue were suspended for the telemedicine doctors, who were expected to forego some of the financial opportunities of traditional practice during the start up phase of the business.

Some grumbling among the doctors about possible income loss was challenged by the angel investor, who said, "Welcome to entrepreneurship; don't do this if you expect to be paid like a regular doctor." From an enterprise standpoint close tracking of patient care volume and revenue was critical to assess how Medi-Tel was faring according to the projections established in the business plan.

An Electronic Medical Record system was chosen from a vendor who committed to help the telemedicine practice customize the software with specialty-specific templates for documentation of assessments and treatments. Since an important aspect of the practice would involve response to emergency situations, an interface was written to link scheduling software to the documentation section so that time of initial contact, time to first contact with a physician, and time to finalize and sign medical records were tracked.

1. Grumble and challenge. Good idea. Challenge will lead to solving a problem ... or will put a grumble to bed!
2. Challenge as soon as you hear a grumble. Failure to challenge quickly can turn grumbles into growls from many.
3. An interface was successfully written? Did anyone get the name and address of that vendor?

Requirement 2D: Alter and test work procedures for altered processes

> Mind-Clearing Example – Imagine an actor who asks for written copies of the Director's instructions and notes for playing an assigned part and hearing the Director say, "Oh, I don't have time to write those down; I'll give you a heads-up if I see you doing something wrong."

Organizations use procedures to guide workers through work processes. A procedure is nothing more than a written set of instructions that describes what workers do for each step of a work process. In the organizations we have worked with over the years, we have found the widest possible range of procedures in play ... all the way from heavily-documented, detailed, tightly-controlled work instructions for NASA flight controllers to "scrap paper notes" taped to machine tools in a manufacturing facility.

People in organizations respond to procedures ... regardless of the form or rigor of the procedure. Organization members have learned the organization's way of doing work, and they know from their experience that following those ways matters. Therefore, if an organization is changing its work processes, it must also change its procedures that describe those processes.

Do we really think that organizations that are trying to change would leave old procedures in play? Yep! All the time! We have seen managers describing the new ways they want to see their organizations do business while standing in the same room with procedure manuals that do not reflect those new ways! If you want your organization to change, modify existing procedures to match new processes ... and publicize them. If the work process alterations in the

ROBERT CUYLER, PHD AND DUTCH HOLLAND, PHD

organization have been extensive, consider having worker training classes on the new procedures.

Testing of new procedures is critical to change. The only way we will know that a new procedure will lead to the right results is to test the newly-written procedures with employees from the populations that will be expected to use them. We recommend what we call a split test to get the most useful information about a newly-written procedure. Identify the test population and split it into two test teams.

- Give Team One a thorough briefing on what you were trying to accomplish with the new procedure … and then let them follow the new procedure to get their work done. Watch closely to see that the procedure works.

- Give Team Two no instructions along with the new procedure. Simply ask them to read the procedure and follow the steps. Watch closely to see how this procedure works. All procedures need to be tested under the "no explanation" condition, because procedures will eventually find their way into the hands of people who need to use them but who have had no explanation.

Make sure that the new procedures are identified with an effective or revised date. Also consider some special marking, border, or color that catches the workers' eyes and lets them know that new work instructions are in place.

Writing, modifying and testing the new procedures are the first steps. Marking those procedures as "new" is the next step. The final step with procedures is to ensure that every organization member who is to use the procedures gets copied. The procedures step is not complete until we know that every affected worker has the needed work instructions in hand.

Think about this: if a Director is moving his cast of twenty actors to a new play, how many copies of the new script does she need? Twenty. How many different folks need to get a copy? Twenty. How does she ensure that each actor has a copy? She hands out twenty on a personal level, or has the Stage Manager issue them and get signatures. How many signatures? Twenty. This ain't rocket science … but it is thorough, detailed, organizational change!

Northwest Memorial Example:
Alter and test work procedures

A team of schedulers from the hub hospital and rural hospital surgical departments working with an outside "scheduling guru" from the EMR Vendor developed new work processes for the scheduling of surgeries to accommodate pre- and post-op telemedicine consultations, as well as scheduling the surgeries themselves from the rural hospitals.

These new scheduling processes were run in parallel with current ways of scheduling so that the differences and potential impacts of change to the new scheduling processes could be observed. The results of the testing were presented to the System surgical nurse manager who in turn presented the procedures to the Telemedicine steering committee and surgical section chief and then to the hospital's medical council for official approval.

DID YOU NOTICE

1. An outside guru on a hot subject area can really be helpful to:
   a. Provide vital "how to do it" information,
   b. Give management increased credibility while taking some of the heat off internal management.
2. Use the outside guru like a rifle, not like a scatter gun: specific set target, defined scope, and required, written deliverable

Medi-Tel Example: Alter and test work procedures

A potential customer, Amax Support, agreed to contract with Medi-Tel for a pilot project that would help establish the logistics of telemedicine care. This customer sent civilian contractors to Iraq and Afghanistan for a variety of military support roles. Returning personnel were brought a central location in the US post-deployment for debriefing. As it was common for medical concerns to be identified at this point, the company asked Medi-Tel to do a comprehensive medical exam within two days of return.

In preparation, Medi-Tel brought in two of Amax's clinic nurses for training as telepresenters. The nurses were trained in Medi-Tel's telemedicine exam rooms to thoroughly learn the operation of all of the medical devices as well as to be directed by each of the specialists on how to examine patients at the direction of the doctor, who would not be able to physically touch a patient. At the end of the training, a model clinical examination for each specialty or procedure was filmed and archived for training purposes to assist in the training of future tele-presenters.

DID YOU NOTICE

1. Did you notice that these guys "didn't waste a drop."
2. They designed a model exam and then filmed it. What easy leverage! Bravo!

Requirement 2E: Eliminate old measures, goals, objectives and procedures

> **Mind-Clearing Example – Imagine a Director who allows the master stage copy of the last production script to remain open and in place right beside the master copy of the new play that is currently being performed. When asked about keeping the copy from the old play, imagine the Director saying, "No, don't move it … you never know when we might need it again!"**

You will be happy to know that commercial airline pilots have mastered change when it comes to new approach procedures. First of all, an approach procedure is a kind of work process that pilots use in approaching an airport for landing. Each airport approach is described in a written procedure that pilots carry with them in the cockpit. Following those procedures to the letter is critical for aircraft safety.

Airports periodically change their approaches to reflect needs for better aircraft routing or safety. When they make such a change, new approach procedures are designed, dated, printed, and distributed to all pilots who will use that airport. A standard part of the physical issuance of the new procedures calls for the pilots to turn in their old procedures first before they can get new ones! This step is designed to ensure that old, out-of-date procedures will not be used past the effective date of the new ones. Why? Because old procedures left around will get used.

Bottom line, the last critical step in altering work processes for organizational change is to get old work process maps, old procedures, old performance goals out of existence. How do you do that? You systematically collect them and then permanently dispose of them ... trash them, shred them, or burn them!

In some situations, where changing to new procedures is especially vital, you might consider holding a formal ceremony to dispose of the old procedures. We have on several occasions worked with clients that had a wake or funeral for old procedures ... to call special attention to the need to move on to the new way of doing business. While this kind of dramatic step may not be needed for organizations that have mastered change, such steps are clearly important for organizations that are just beginning to become proficient at change. I can see it now ... a leader looking over the flames of an old procedure pyre into the eyes of employees mourning the loss of that last crib sheet for getting their job done ... and seeing them take a deep breath to move on to the new way of doing business!

Northwest Memorial Example: Eliminate Old Measures, Goals, Objectives and Procedures

Out with the old, or the old will stay the norm. The old procedures for surgical scheduling were collected and trashed. Along with the old procedures, the Chief Nursing Officer worked with two senior surgical department members and a representative of IT and the EMR Vendor to write down what they knew to be "unwritten procedures" that were being used in the affected surgical departments. Old procedures along with the list of unwritten procedures were officially retired at an all-hands meeting of the departments. Additional unwritten procedures were identified at this department meeting by asking department members, "what other unwritten ways of doing business need to also be retired."

The Mobile Crisis Team discarded the old Policy and Procedure manual for psychiatric emergencies, including home office copies which would be referred to during evening and weekend coverage.

ROBERT CUYLER, PHD AND DUTCH HOLLAND, PHD

1. Did you see the special attention to taking out the trash?
2. Old trash lying around is the same as World War II hand grenades brought back from the war!

And in conclusion ...

Process steps are used to build things, to make something out of nothing, and without processes there would be no organizational outcomes. Implementation of a telemedicine practice cannot occur until a healthcare organization's existing processes and procedures are physically altered to accommodate the new direction. In this chapter we focused on changing the physical steps the organization uses to get its work done to ensure that a new way of operating will be possible in the future.

The step of transitioning work processes to enable the change vision is perhaps the most important step to get right. Very careful attention must be paid to the validity of the process steps that will make up the new way of doing business. Changing processes and procedures is not enough, however. Most work processes call for the use of tools, equipment, software, etc., a vital subject to be covered in the next chapter.

CHAPTER FOUR

Alter Facilities, Equipment, and Technology (FET)

Mind-Clearing Example – Imagine a Director who fails to make arrangements to rent the theater for the new production. Or who fails to commission workmen to transfer the set and stage rigging from the configuration of the last play to the new one!

AN ORGANIZATION CANNOT reach its vision for change unless the facilities, equipment, and technology (FET) needed to support changed work processes has been altered, tested and made available to trained employees. That is an absolute requirement. In addition, the vision will not be realized until the old FET that is not to be used after the transition has been destroyed and removed from the workplace.

Our task in this chapter is to focus on the third requirement for transitioning an organization: the physical alteration of the organization's FET. Every organizational change is likely to require new or altered FET of some kind to enable the altered work processes designed to fulfill the vision. Regardless of the kind of organizational change or the stimulus for organizational change, we work with the assumption that FET alterations will be required ... unless proven otherwise.

As fast bandwidth has become ubiquitous and device cost/capability has improved exponentially, tele-health activity has exploded in variety and usage. The cost of business-grade video-conference systems with the capability of running medical peripheral devices has shrunk, placing equipment within reach of health systems and practitioners that had previously been dependent on grant sources for infrastructure. However, grant sources continue to support innovative programs as well as subsidizing infrastructure, such as USDA's support of bandwidth for rural hospitals. Reimbursement for telemedicine services has been incremental and spotty. Medicare has recognized telemedicine to rural health settings for well over a decade. Medicaid telemedicine policy, which is administered at the State level, varies considerably. Commercial payers are required to cover telemedicine, at least to some extent, in 13 states. Evolving health systems, such as Accountable Care Organizations, are expected to embrace telemedicine more fully as a means to improve access and outcomes.

The introduction of smart phones puts significant computing power in the palm of the hand, creating a pathway and marketplace for health-related applications that is vastly cheaper and faster than traditional health technology patterns. A quick scan of smart phone applications shows offerings in smoking cessation, dermatology, radiology, diabetes management, psychiatry, and cardiology. These offerings, which are often labeled M-Health, may offer services directly to a consumer (e.g., self-help or self-monitoring of diet or mood), or may connect a consumer to a doctor (e.g., Iphone photo of suspicious moles read remotely by a dermatologist), or may allow a physician to review and evaluate medical data remotely (e.g., FDA-approved radiology viewer).

While medical applications that live on smart phones navigate innovative but uncharted waters, the increasing deployment of telemedicine in mainstream settings (hospitals, clinics, and doctor's offices) has been facilitated by the availability and affordability of business-grade video-conference systems which can be enhanced by the integration of medical-grade peripheral devices such as digital stethoscopes, general examination cameras, ophthalmoscopes, and otoscopes. Adoption of industry standards for interoperability ensures that equipment from different manufacturers can connect with one another over the open internet, assuming firewall adjustments are made to networks to allow external traffic.

Concerning medical records, the practice of telemedicine is greatly enhanced by the availability of electronic records which can be remotely generated and accessed by the practitioner and available as well at the patient care side. However, as of the time of this writing, the healthcare system in the United States is in the midst of a massive conversion to Electronic Health Records, with a mix of financial incentives and penalties driving physician conversion from paper records to EMR's. As EMR availability remains partial, the combinations

ROBERT CUYLER, PHD AND DUTCH HOLLAND, PHD

and permutations of telemedicine medical record management are multiple. Although there is considerable Federal emphasis for interoperable medical records, the reality remains that proprietary systems do not readily or easily exchange health information amongst one another.

The more complex the access and exchange of data is, the more practitioner workflow is compromised, which can easily discourage doctors from participation in telemedicine. By default, many telemedicine projects continue to rely on faxed or mailed paper documents because of the unavailability or complexity of true electronic exchange. This is particularly the case when the telemedicine entity and the patient-care side are not part of the same organization or healthcare system. Unlike the often seamless interoperability of H.323-based videoconference systems, the coordination of medical records systems between the doctor- and patient-sides is significantly more complex.

Schedules may be integrated into or separate from EMR's. Electronic management of schedules requires that both sides of the telemedicine encounter have access. Policies and procedures must establish the process for making, changing, or cancelling appointments. Doctors are often reluctant to allow outside entities the permission to schedule their time, so physician practice personnel may communicate with the patient-side by phone or email to manage scheduling. In this book, we will address the importance of understanding and managing workflow; while decidedly unglamorous, physician scheduling is a key ingredient in the viability of many telemedicine initiatives.

We have certainly seen organizational changes that required little or no alteration in FET. As a simple example, imagine a home construction contractor who does lumber framing. Changing the place the frames are put together (e.g., at the job site or at the lumber yard) will require major alterations in work steps but require no changes in the hammers used by the framing carpenters. On the other hand, this same framing contractor might need to change the equipment used to haul the completed, bulky frames to the job site.

Just as work process steps and procedures go together, FET and operating guidelines go together. Operating guidelines are the written instructions for proper use and operation of FET, be it a ladder, a piece of earth moving equipment or new EMR software. Failing to provide proper operating guidelines for new or altered FET is akin to expecting a new look from a play that is opening with the old set and old costumes left over from the last play.

Change requires FET alterations

The obvious case for altering FET comes when new FET is the organization's change focus from the beginning (e.g., "Our goal is to implement EMR"). Other cases requiring alterations of FET are driven by very different kinds of change motivations. For example:

- If a healthcare organization decides to change its business strategy to become the low cost provider, many, if not all, of the organization's delivery processes will need to change to take out costly steps or to alter the sequence of steps. Altering any parts of the work process is likely to require a different facility configuration and changed support systems.

- If an organization decides to re-engineer one of its work processes in order to achieve new efficiencies or a new level of safe operation, changes might be required in everything from guard rails to shut-off switches to healthcare product assembly lines. As FET changes are made, corresponding changes will be needed in the written operating guidelines that support the FET changes.

- If an organization decides to make a change in its culture (e.g., with culture simply defined as "the way we do things around here"), several process changes will result as organization members begin to approach their jobs differently. If for example, the desired cultural change is to become more attentive to customers, changes will probably need to be made in the steps used in customer service departments or help desks. As alterations are made in customer service steps, modifications are likely to be required in the tools used by customer service employees, namely software applications and telecommunications equipment.

The Requirement to alter the organization's FET is both one of the "best handled" components of organizational change and one of the worst. For what we call "visible FET,"—physical plant, medical devices, and wheel chairs—alterations are usually very well done for the transition to a new way of operating. We think this kind of change is handled so well because these technologies are visible and easy to see … failure to alter this kind of FET would be easy to spot and correct.

But when the FET to be altered is not easy to see, it is frequently not handled as well. For example, alteration of software to enable changes that need to be made in work processes seems much tougher to deal with for several reasons. For example, software is usually changed by specialists in back rooms; such activity is not easy to

ROBERT CUYLER, PHD AND DUTCH HOLLAND, PHD

see and, therefore, workers are unlikely to see what is going on or what is coming. Even though software changes have been announced as being underway, it is frequently a surprise when workers come in to work to find "new computer screens" associated with their job. In addition, FET that needs to be added to support core FET is often overlooked or poorly handled. For example, changing the customer service software application for a help center might be completed on target, but the new telecommunication equipment for workers using that new software may be forgotten. You are kidding. No, it happens. (Our approach for dealing with the software alteration issue is covered in a later section of this chapter.)

Identify and dispel deadly assumptions that will disable FET transition

The step of transitioning FET to enable the change vision looks straight-forward. However experience has taught that nothing about change is really a slam-dunk, one-step action. Once again we face deadly assumptions, but this time those assumptions may have a hard-driving, articulate force behind them. FET vendors frequently have mantras they repetitively deliver to your organizations during work time as well as during "lubrication time" spent with your key buyers.

Popular mantras include: "Our software really does do everything! Our stuff is THE complete solution! Once our software goes live, your problem is over, and your work is finished! Implement our solution and you and your department will be the heroes of the change initiative!" Just imagine those sweet words whispered in your ear as you stand, glass of expensive champagne in hand, salt spray in your face, breathing crisp and clear Pacific air, on the bow of the $100M yacht that is expected to win this year's America's Cup. "Ah, this really must be great FET we are buying, and it surely must take care of everything!"

Step	Deadly Assumptions	Disabling Behavior by Management	Proven Consequences
Transitioning FET	1. Once the new FET is "in", the change will be taken care of. 2. The FET (or the vendor) will do everything, just like they said 3. It's just a process change, we don't even need to look at FET.	1. Leaving the FET up to the vendor. 2. Focusing exclusively on technical implementation. 3. Not auditing the impact of FET on processes and roles.	• Frustration • Un-met expectations • Return to use of old FET • Increased apprehension about change

Change leaders can spot the likely presence of deadly assumptions about FET through conversations about what needs to be done to get FET transitioned. Hearing the suggestion to "leave the FET up to the vendor" calls for the change leader to surface deadly assumptions and to dispel them in any way possible, starting with the proven consequences in the table above.

Take These Action Steps to Transition FET

Now we are on to the hard work of transitioning FET using the following five steps. Skip a step and expect expensive delays.

Action steps to transition FET

- 3A: Identify the FET alterations needed for the change
- 3B: Alter and test all FET needed for the change
- 3C: Alter and test each and every FET control
- 3D: Alter or create operating guidelines for all involved FET
- 3E: Eliminate old FET and operating guidelines

Requirement 3A: Identify the FET alterations needed for change

> *Mind-Clearing Example – Imagine a Director who selects a new play and who commits to an opening date without planning the modifications that will be needed for the props and backdrops for staging the new play.*

The FET part of transitioning an organization to a new way of operating starts with the identification of the FET that will be impacted by the transition. To have any hope of making an organization successfully change, we must know, with as much certainty as possible, the construction or alterations tasks that must be completed before the FET transition can be completed.

This step to identify needed FET alterations can be anything from a huge project in itself (if the vision includes merging with another hospital) to a short and sweet exercise (if the acquisition is something as simple as adding new IV pumps with more time-saving features). We have been successful in identifying needed alterations to an organization's FET with two different approaches … the FET inventory approach and the process inventory approach. The FET Inventory approach is the most logical to use when the organizational change is

ROBERT CUYLER, PHD AND DUTCH HOLLAND, PHD

being driven primarily by the desire for new FET such as a new MRI, additional clinic space, or a new software application. The process inventory approach is the most logical for all other kinds of organizational changes.

Approach One: The FET Inventory approach. This approach calls for examination of each element of FET that is connected to a major FET change. For example, a hospital may have to get new light speed CT equipment because the speed of their existing out-of-date equipment is causing service delays. Installing new FET almost always starts a ripple effect of needed work on existing FET to physically accommodate the new major FET change. For example the new CT mentioned above may require a change in the room layout or the electrical power.

Approach Two: The process inventory approach. This approach calls for examination of each work process change that is contemplated, looking for the use of FET in any process step. Use of this approach to identify needed alterations in FET assumes that the reason for the organizational change is something other than major FET driven. Many alterations in FET are needed because the organization starts out to change its strategy, work processes, or the behavior and performance of its employees. For example, what if a hospital strategy is to distinguish the patient experience by providing on-demand room service to their patients? This strategy would require retooling the kitchen to operate more like a short order restaurant, providing extra room and technology for a call center to take orders based on diet restrictions, as well as facilities close to the patient rooms for the servers to prep and deliver the meal in their formal attire.

Regardless of the inventory approach that is chosen, the bottom line fact associated with the installation and lifetime value of new FET is very simple. It is very easy and commonplace to overlook changes that are needed in existing FET to accommodate the new FET. Over the years, we have seen many organizational changes delayed because the transition to needed FET had an unexpected and un-planned ripple effect on neighboring equipment. We have seen unanticipated power drains that impact other equipment; we have seen many heating and cooling problems emerge because of new equipment operating in ways different than it was planned, and so on.

The results of a FET inventory: The kinds of alterations that could appear on a FET alteration team's list might be as follows:

- Cut pass-through window between specimen receiving and processing areas
- Add three more centrifuges for running smaller, faster turnaround specimen batches
- Upgrade electronic interface so that results can post on the electronic patient record and alert the ordering unit when critical values have been exceeded.

In reality, a FET alteration team will need to repeat the inventory step at least two more times: during the installation of the newly-acquired FET and after installation is complete. Our experience over thirty years is that additional needed alterations in an organization's existing FET will continue to be found right through installation and use ... and sometimes even months or years later!

A special case: the acquisition of telemedicine technology

Project planners in telemedicine will invariably become involved in identifying and choosing the video-conference systems on which clinical care will be delivered. The range of possible systems and price-points from which to choose can be staggering. Establishing a video connection between a doctor and patient can span free or low cost consumer-grade systems that run on PC's and tablets to 'tele-presence' systems that can run to six figures per side. While telemedicine planners or coordinators may learn about systems and features from trade shows, manufacturer web sites or recommendations from other organizations, the due diligence process should involve meetings with vendors, whether video-conference or telemedicine companies themselves or re-sellers, followed by visits to vendor customers without the vendor in attendance.

The nature of the medical care being delivered will have substantial impact on the type of system to be considered. Cognitive-based examination or consultation, such as in psychiatry, may run effectively on business-grade video-conference systems with effective data security features. Put more simply, some forms of telemedicine can be provided by linking "two talking heads."

More complex medical care may involve a variety of peripheral devices that facilitate examination, including digital cameras, examination scopes, stethoscopes, and other vital sign monitoring devices. Project managers therefore need to make a careful assessment of the present and future telemedicine applications under consideration in order to begin an effective process for considering features, performance, and costs of potential telemedicine systems. The managers also need to make an assessment of the organization's readiness to implement telemedicine in order to understand the internal factors that will facilitate or hinder the effective launch and support of the telemedicine services. We recommend the following 'internal look' in order to inform the vendor search to follow.

Internal Questions:

1. Is senior management of the hospital/organization aware of the telemedicine project? What is the level of senior management input and buy-in? Are there stake-holders in the system who may be key proponents or opponents of the project?

2. Is the telemedicine initiative consistent with the key strategic directions of the organization?

3. Has a preliminary budget addressed capital costs, technical support costs, and training/ancillary costs? Have expected revenue sources and volumes (and regulatory issues) been adequately researched and estimated?

4. Is the telemedicine project expected to address a single or multiple specialties? What peripheral devices might be needed to support specialty care?

5. What is the level of IT sophistication within the organization? Does IT have background/experience in telemedicine? Does IT have experience/background in system integration, with the capability of integrating peripheral medical devices into the telemedicine infrastructure? Does IT have the available personnel to commit to the design and launch of the telemedicine project? Has Senior Management directed IT to give the necessary priority and resources to the telemedicine initiative?

6. Are there other major technology change initiatives underway or on the horizon (e.g., Electronic Medical Record) that are commanding the attention and resources of the organization?

7. Are a project manager and team on board to design and manage the project from blueprint stage to implementation?

Once these internal factors are understood and documented, the organization is in a position to shift attention to telemedicine equipment and vendor selection. The nature of telemedicine projects typically will involve an ongoing relationship between the purchasing organization and the maker / vendor, because the working relationship with a vendor or re-seller can be as important as the hardware itself.

What follows is guidance on important questions to ask a potential video-conference / telemedicine equipment vendor.

Vendor Questions:

1. Do you offer a single manufacturer's telemedicine equipment or options from multiple makers?

2. Are your preferred video-conference vendors active in supplying healthcare organizations with telemedicine technology? If so, for how many years and with what type of organizations and medical specialties?

3. Given the type of telemedicine services we expect to deliver, can you demonstrate how your products and services match our performance/price needs? Can you break down initial fixed costs versus recurring costs?

4. How do you address data security and patient privacy in healthcare applications?

5. How can you scale your products and services to help us manage our existing project and anticipated growth?

6. What additional implementation features and costs should we expect as telemedicine services grow?

7. Describe your company's approach to linking video-conference systems to other devices (computers, tablets, mobile phones). How can infrequent users be linked without the need for dedicated equipment?

8. Describe your company's approach to inter-operability and flexibility. Does your company rely on standards-based or proprietary connectivity?

ROBERT CUYLER, PHD AND DUTCH HOLLAND, PHD

9. Do your systems run on a closed-network basis? If so, how can callers from outside of the core network be added?

10. Describe ease-of-use features for both end users (e.g., doctors or nurses) and IT personnel.

11. Describe your company's warranty and service-level agreements? What is and is not supported in your agreements?

12. Can you provide and support integrated telemedicine peripheral devices, either within your company or in collaboration with system integrators or telemedicine vendors who use your video-conference platform?

13. How can your company's systems be used for business communication and training in addition to clinical care? Do you have systems for recording and streaming video? Can you describe how such recorded content can be accessed?

14. Describe how your products provide multi-point capacity? What are the additional costs for adding multi-point calls?

Establishing a clear understanding of internal needs and resources is critical to making good matches between organization and telemedicine technology. We contend that the internal assessment described above is an essential step to prepare the organization to review the options available in the marketplace.

One of the interesting aspects of telemedicine is that sophisticated, well-resourced organizations are often providing services to under-resourced organizations that may lack the same degree of IT and operational capabilities. The ultimate success of the endeavor can depend heavily on the front-end analysis and planning that matches price, features, ease-of-use, and support needs to the characteristics of all of the telemedicine participants.

A very special case: the alteration or acquisition of software

For the purposes of this book, we will consider software to be FET ... a very important part of FET. It is a rare organizational change these days that does not involve some information technology system. Everything that we have said so far about altering FET applies to software/systems. But many times the organization members who get involved in the alteration of FET are different when software is involved ... that's the good news ... and the bad news!

When we talk to information FET professionals about "altering" software, they immediately translate what we are saying into the vocabulary of their profession. Their translation becomes "application development or application sourcing." In many organizations there are Information Technology (IT) professionals who specialize in "apps" or "applications development" (AD). These professionals already have approaches or techniques they use to develop, modify or acquire an IT application. The first step in their usual approach is frequently called "defining requirements." Depending on the size of your organization, you may have IT professionals who specialize in defining requirements for applications development or sourcing. And therein lies both the good news and the bad news.

We have found it very difficult to intervene in a requirements definition process. Most IT professionals who do requirements definition are focused professionals using a disciplined approach to identify and record what users want their new or modified information system to do. That's the good news ... a professional using a systematic approach can come help you with the identification of the alterations that will be needed to your software FET.

The bad news is that frequently the IT professional does not receive a really good picture of the organizational change that is driving the system alteration (i.e., the implementation of a telemedicine practice). This inadequate or incomplete picture can occur because the users who are interviewed by the IT professional do not have or convey a good picture of the vision ... or because of the narrow focus of the IT professional who is only listening for technical "entering arguments" to the applications development/sourcing process. These entering arguments can be way off base because of a lack of understanding of the business and a lack of understanding of the new way of doing business being contemplated.

Never give up on steering the IT end of the organizational change. Use the old rule, "Expect what you inspect," and what you should see next will be altered software that helps you keep your organizational change on target, on time, and on budget!

Northwest Memorial Example:
Identify the FET alterations needed for change

The most important FET change was to equip two of the rural hospitals with dedicated high-bandwidth internet connections

ROBERT CUYLER, PHD AND DUTCH HOLLAND, PHD

for telemedicine, as the existing System T-1 lines were over-subscribed with regular usage. In the process of diagnosing 'frozen' video calls, the rural hospital IT departments discovered that staff personal usage of the internet for streaming video and music during work hours was placing a significant strain on usable bandwidth. Adjustments to firewalls as well as sternly-worded reminders from the CEO about personal internet usage were implemented to conserve bandwidth for approved uses.

In cardiology, digital stethoscopes from three vendors were tested, and the preferred devices were purchased and configured in designated consult rooms at each of the rural hospital outpatient clinics.

DID YOU NOTICE

1. Taking care of IT includes requiring behavioral changes, i.e., managing personal usages.
2. Test, test, and test!

Medi-Tel Example: Identify the FET alterations/acquisitions needed for change

As the telemedicine doctors would be practicing in front of cameras and monitors, the optimal design of their exam rooms was radically different from that of traditional rooms. A contractor was brought in re-design the doctors' offices to center around the telemedicine equipment. Lighting and sound-proofing changes were made to adjust to the needs of telemedicine. As 24 hour crisis availability was built into the company's offerings, specs for sleeping quarters and a shower for doctors on call were sent to the professional building contractor for design and cost estimates. For services at the customer location, a lockable telemedicine cart was designed to incorporate the primary camera as well as all of the peripheral medical devices.

Discussions of coverage and provider expansion led to a realization that the team had underestimated the need for physician coverage from a variety of locations. Equipment for home offices and for mobile solutions that could be moved from location to location were not factored into the original business plan, thereby significantly underestimating infrastructure costs. Medi-Tel arranged additional meetings with the primary telemedicine equipment vendor, who was challenged to design a physician telemedicine studio that could fit in a hardened suitcase. This device design would allow doctors to practice from a home office or any other location with adequate internet bandwidth. As this was a customized solution, estimated costs were significantly higher than the 'off-the-shelf' equipment which was to be the standard solution. Input was sought from the Advisory Board member with banking/healthcare background to factor the new costs into the business plan as well as to discuss options for financing these capital costs.

DID YOU NOTICE

1. The company underestimated needs and therefore costs. Wow! What do you think that did to investor confidence?
2. What to do?
   a. Go visit multiple telemedicine businesses. Look, ask, and learn.
   b. Hire a "fishing guide" who has been down this river before and who knows where the fish are!

Requirement 3B: Alter/Acquire and test FET critical for the change

Mind-Clearing Example – Imagine a Stage Manager who receives the Director's list of the needed scenery changes for the new play, but who tells the puzzled stagehands "not to change anything" from the last play: "Just give it a new coat of paint," he says.

Or imagine the Lighting Director (1) asking an electrical technician if all the spotlights had been changed to the new required colors and (2) being happy with the following answer, "Yes, kinda, I changed three of the five, and they switch on most of the time."

By this time the change leader should have clearly identified both the new FET needed for the impending change and the alterations that will be needed to existing FET. In this step, the change leader now needs to ensure that all the needed FET work gets done satisfactorily. In addition, he must ensure that all new and altered FET has been thoroughly tested to ensure that it operates as it needs to in order to support the Vision.

To a large degree, the change leader's success in making needed alterations in FET will be dependent on his organization's capability in two important management areas: construction management and software management. Getting needed alteration of FET (not software) will be dependent on how well the organization executes management principles as applied to the acquisition and/or construction of FET. Getting needed alterations of software FET will largely be dependent on the organization's maturity or development level in software processes.

Alteration of physical FET (i.e., "Bricks")

Consider this kind of alteration as a "construction project." For physical FET some form of the discipline of management as applied to FET acquisition must be used to have any chance of successfully installing new FET or altering existing FET (assuming that we are talking about something more than going to a hardware store and picking up a new claw hammer).

The change leaders in the organization must themselves have a "common sense construction management mindset." Almost every manager in today's organizations has at least some passing experience with FET or equipment purchase and/or installation (i.e., building or installing something), or they are veterans of construction projects around their homes. They may have been assigned to manage a simple construction project (re-modeling an office or buying and installing a new cabinet in the break room) or they have been around while such a project was being worked.

Change leaders can get construction management in play in FET alteration in any of three different ways … and their choice of a way or approach should be based on the size and complexity of the needed FET alteration.

- **Use Common Sense Construction Management**. For small or simple purchases or installations, it may be OK to use nothing more than the common sense approach … but it must be done in a very disciplined way … with goals, budgets, and schedules and so on.

- **Engage an internal manager who is experienced in Construction Management**. Acquiring or building FET is not new for most organizations that have a history of change and/or expansion. Many organizations have qualified professionals on board who can become the acquisition manager for acquiring and/altering FET associated with organizational change.

- **Engage a professional management company (or professional) from the outside** for facility construction changes if knowledge is not resident in-house. Some organizations prefer to use outside construction resources for large and/or complicated processes. You may be aware that there is an entire industry called "Engineering and Construction" whose mission it is to design, procure, and construct major capital projects for healthcare.

Alteration/acquisition of Software FET (i.e., "Clicks")

The process of buying, developing or modifying software FET will usually be handled by the organization's Information Technology Department. IT Departments in most companies are accustomed to handling such changes. But from our perspective, what counts is the IT Department's overall competence in handling software change in an orderly predictable way that will allow transition projects to be on target, on time, and on budget.

The Software Engineering Institute of Carnegie Mellon University talks about the overall capability of IT organizations to manage software processes. They talk about IT organizations that are "immature" versus those that are "mature."

> "In an immature software organization, software processes are generally improvised by practitioners and their management during the course of the project. Even if a software process has been specified, it is not rigorously followed or enforced. The immature software organization is reactionary, and managers are usually focused on solving immediate crises (better known as fire-fighting). Schedules and budgets are routinely exceeded because they are not based on realistic estimates. When hard deadlines are imposed, product functionality and quality are often compromised to meet the schedule.

ROBERT CUYLER, PHD AND DUTCH HOLLAND, PHD

"On the other hand, a mature software organization possesses an organization-wide ability for managing software development and maintenance processes. The software process is accurately communicated to both existing staff and new employees, and work activities are carried out according to the planned process. The processes mandated are fit for use and consistent with the way the work actually gets done. These defined processes are updated when necessary, and improvements are developed through controlled pilot-tests and/or cost benefit analyses. Roles and responsibilities within the defined process are clear throughout the project and across the organization.

"In a mature organization, managers monitor the quality of the software products and customer satisfaction ... schedules and budgets are based on historical performance and are realistic; the expected results for cost, schedule, functionality, and quality of the product are usually achieved." (Technical Report SEI-93-TR-24)

In our quest to make changes happen on target, on time, and on budget, it is easy to see how alteration of FET might be a weak link in organizational change if those alterations were being done by an IT organization with immature software processes. Our recommendations for handling different levels of maturity and different degrees of needed alteration are shown in very general form in the following table:

Software Alterations

		Simple and Small	Big and Complex
IT Organization	Mature	Use in-house IT resources	Consider using in-house IT resources supplemented by mature outside vendor
	Immature	Do with in-house resources only if you use the best IT performers	Use mature outside vendor only

Figure 6.1 Recommendations for Resourcing Software Alteration

The chart above is probably clear enough to send the strong message that IT maturity is a requirement for altering software that is to be a part of an organizational change intended to be on target, on time, and on budget. One point of explanation might be useful for simple, small changes done in-house in an immature IT organization. For this case, it is very important to get the very best IT resources in the organization on the software alteration project. Odds are they will not use systematic software processes ... but they probably will do the best job in the IT organization of improvising the software solution.

Testing new and altered FET

Just as we tested altered work processes in an earlier transition step, we must test new or altered FET to ensure that it will be ready to play its part in the organizational change. If the key principles are used in altering the physical FET, testing of the final FET and its installation will be done as a part of the project close out. Sounds like an easy-enough answer to our testing requirement, doesn't it?

Beware of the testing done at the close out of the project ... whether it be for physical or software FET. Those are needed tests, and they likely will be done right as part of a disciplined alteration, but they don't go far enough. What is needed here are tests of the FET in the context of the <u>actual</u> work processes that require those particular tools. Our recommendation here is to use members of the work process alteration and FET alteration teams to conduct a real-life test of the FET using the altered processes defined earlier. A further step would be to use employees who will actually be using the FET (and not just the "super users") with the altered process when the intended change is finally put into effect.

Tests of the altered FET almost always produce observations from the test participants that point to the need for further alterations of the FET. Change leaders will need to differentiate between those suggested alterations that are learning-curve based or preferences/styles-based rather than process-requirements based. Learning curve based suggestions may be driven more by the test subjects' unfamiliarity with the FET than with actual FET inadequacy. If we discover major needed alterations at this point ... we haven't been doing something right!

Northwest Memorial Example:
Alter and Test FET Critical for the Change

IT technicians installed and configured telemedicine cameras in multiple locations at the Northwest hub (surgery, psychiatry, and cardiology) and at the rural hospital outpatient clinics and Emergency Departments. Telemedicine software compatible with the cameras was installed on secure laptops assigned to the Mobile Crisis Team for after-hours coverage, and an additional laptop was configured for the on-call psychiatrists to run from home offices during their rotating call weeks.

DID YOU NOTICE

1. Think through all the details and get all the technical work done before workers begin to work with the equipment to lessen frustration and resistance.
2. Never start training on a piece of equipment that has not been bullet-proof tested.
3. "Oh, this particular piece of equipment has not been configured yet, so just imagine …," is a deadly phrase that can set back an entire implementation.

Medi-Tel Example:
Alter and Test FET Critical for the Change

A prototype telemedicine cart was delivered to the Medi-Tel facilities, and the system was installed and configured by the IT Director. Representatives of the medical peripheral devices were invited in one-by-one to test and calibrate the devices and to deliver detailed operational instructions for routine use and trouble-shooting. The stethoscope and examination camera were sources of considerable debate among the physicians regarding ease of use and clinical quality, as the systems with the best ergonomics did not necessarily provide the clearest sounds or images.

The physicians who were more 'generalists' voted for ergonomics, as they believed that workflow and reduced risk of error would be enhanced by devices which had simple interfaces. The 'purists' among the specialists wanted signal quality over anything else and maintained that systematic training would bring all users to the same level of competence. Vendors agreed to provide demo units for testing in a variety of settings until the physicians reached a consensus.

1. The physicians had different points of view and preferences. How is that for a revelation?
2. Arranging for the demo units is about the best way to handle different preferences. Use demo units and time to let nature take its course. Bravo.

Requirement 3C: Alter and test FET controls

> *Mind-Clearing Example – Imagine a Lighting Director who ensures that all the right lights are in place and focused on the stage but who does not alter or test the lighting "control panel" that is still set up for the last production!*

So far we have altered work processes and purchased/altered and tested the FET required for use in those altered processes. In this step, the change leader's job is to ensure that the controls on the FET will allow the performance called for by the work process. FET controls are those devices that allow the operators of the FET to make the equipment do what it needs to do, when it needs to do it, in order to perform the work called for by work processes. Sometimes limitations have been set on FET controls that limit the overall performance of the FET.

A simple real-world example of FET control might be the accelerator pedal on a truck. Some trucks have a device called a governor installed on the engine. A governor artificially limits the engine speed of the truck to some speed well within the truck's operating limits. If that truck is moved to the kind of work that requires a higher speed than the one set on the governor, the truck driver will not be able to drive the truck to meet work process goals.

The job of the change leader is to ensure that control devices on altered equipment are adjusted to meet new process requirements, and that control devices on new equipment provide the operating envelope needed by the work processes. While the FET tests in the previous step will pick up control limitations on the specific FET tested, all duplicate equipment will need to be physically inspected to ensure it is set within the needed operating parameters.

Northwest Memorial Example:
Alter and test FET controls

The Telemedicine Coordinator took responsibility for creating individualized dialing directories for all of the telemedicine cameras to make certain that all of the potential call sites were programmed into each machine.

IT assisted all of the psychiatrists to configure and test equipment for evening/weekend call. One of the psychiatrists needed to upgrade home internet speed, and all of the doctors were advised to use hard-wired rather than wireless connections to optimize call quality. The telepsychiatry 'champion' agreed to orient and competency-test all of his colleagues on providing and documenting emergency psychiatric assessments to Emergency Departments.

DID YOU NOTICE

1. Altering and testing was done for each physician by the trained expert. It's just like hand-holding, right? It is hand-holding and that is exactly what is required!
2. The champion agreed to orient and test colleagues. Handle with care, but it is just better if done doc to doc.
3. Equipment and controls are the easy part ... there is no excuse for not getting this right!

Medi-Tel Example: Alter and test FET controls

A prototype telemedicine cart was delivered to the logistical support company that agreed to the pilot project. Medi-Tel's IT director traveled to their location to supervise installation and configuration of the cart and to stage testing of the peripheral medical devices. He purposely stayed somewhat in the background and assisted the on-site IT personnel to determine the likely level of assistance that clients would need when they received equipment.

Once the video-conference camera was working, Dr. Janssen oriented the company's nursing staff to 'tele-presenting' and did the first testing of the peripheral devices in the hands of the non-

physician staff who would be typical users at the distant site. It was soon apparent that the devices with best signal quality but less user-friendly interfaces would present major difficulties in ordinary clinical use. Since the non-physician 'tele-presenters' would have to handle the devices in examining patients (at the direction of the Medi-Tel physician), ease of use and standard-of-care medical quality would be preferable to a device which was somewhat better but potentially introduce errors or uncertainty into examinations because of overly-complicated interfaces. Dr. Janssen brought the field-trial information back to the medical group and reached a consensus on device choice.

DID YOU NOTICE

1. Testing isn't really testing unless the people who will do the work are in on it.
2. Having the boss lead the test was a homerun! Having the vender do the test was an option, but not a good one. Bravo!

Requirement 3D: Alter or create operating guidelines for all involved FET

> *Mind-Clearing Example – Imagine a Stage Director who refuses to allow his lighting technicians to put new-equipment operating limitations down on paper. Imagine the Lighting Director saying, "Don't worry about writing all this stuff down, we will just remember it."*

Organizations use operating guidelines to guide workers through the proper use of FET. An operating guideline is nothing more than a written set of instructions that describes what workers should and should not do in operation of a particular piece of FET. Operating guidelines are usually provided by the original equipment manufacturers (OEM) of the FET. Operating guidelines are not the same as procedures for work processes.

To avoid any confusion between the two terms, let's look at an example of

ROBERT CUYLER, PHD AND DUTCH HOLLAND, PHD

operating guidelines for simple equipment and the work procedures that use that equipment

- The copier in our office had the following **operating guidelines** attached to the top of the machine:

  1. Do not replenish toner before the "Add Toner" lamp flashes
  2. When replenishing toner, add only one cartridge of toner.

- Meanwhile, we had several **work procedures** that involved the use of that copier:

  1. Take the original of your Expense Form 3440 to the department's Ricoh copier
  2. Enter your department's copier code first (to get a code, contact Wayne at extension 2880)
  3. Make 3 copies of the Expense Form 3440 and return the copies to the admin desk

In the organizations we have worked with over the years, we have found a wide range of operating guidelines in play in work areas. For some FET, we have seen extensive operating guidelines, usually provided by the OEM, available at each machine, and we have also seen the other extreme … three-line operating guidelines in the form of "crib notes" affixed to the equipment itself.

The important thing about operating guidelines is not necessarily how many there are but how usable they are. We have found that most operating guidelines provided by OEM are not only skimpy and poorly-written, but user unfriendly! The exception to this general finding is FET that has a possible loss of life associated with it. In those cases, operating guidelines are much better written and user friendly.

Most companies develop additional operating guidelines beyond those produced by the OEM. Sometimes these additional operating guidelines are written down, but unfortunately, most times they are not. So around existing FET there is frequently an unwritten body of operating guidelines that is important to the organization's knowledge of how to use the FET.

Given this background of poorly written instructions and unwritten guidelines, leaders of a change initiative must still divine a way to make change happen on target, on time and on budget. Therefore, the critical challenges for dealing with FET operating guidelines are as follows:

- **Challenge One: For new FET, supplement the OEM-provided operating guidelines with your organization's standard additions**. This means that the operating guidelines that come with the newly-purchased FET should not be accepted as all that is needed. As a part of the installation and test of the new FET, make it a priority to write additional operating instructions as needed to come up to the standard that your organization already provides on existing FET.

- **Challenge Two: For existing FET that needs to be altered, change the operating guidelines in writing.** If the impending organizational change calls for the modification of existing FET, the task to get operating guidelines in order will be to document the written and unwritten guidelines already in use for the FET before modification – and then re-write those guidelines for the altered equipment. We have found it effective to sometimes write out the new guidelines on the same document with visible "marks through" of the specific guidelines no longer to be used.

Testing of operating guidelines for new FET and altered guidelines for existing FET is critical to change. The only way we will know that new guidelines will lead to the right results is to test the newly-written guidelines with employees from the populations that will be expected to use them. We recommend what we call a split test to get the most useful information about operating guidelines. (See the Split Test in Chapter 2D.)

Make sure that the new operating guidelines are identified with an "effective date" or a "revised date." Also consider some special marking, border, or color that catches the workers' eyes and lets them know that new operating guidelines are in place. Once again, new guidelines are of no value unless we get them into the hands of the people who will need to use them in their day-to-day work.

Northwest Memorial Example: Alter or create operating guidelines for all involved FET

As the intra-organizational telemedicine initiative was formed, the Telemedicine Coordinator assumed responsibility for coordinating all technical support which includes the videoconference cameras, peripheral devises, and EMR.

ROBERT CUYLER, PHD AND DUTCH HOLLAND, PHD

Since the EMR would be fully functional within months of the telemedicine start-up, involvement of the training and technical resources of the EMR vendor was critical. Specific guidelines for telemedicine documentation were developed, since access to medical records at the distant, doctor-side location is a critical aspect of work-flow.

A small team led by the IT Director worked to clarify contractual terms and obligations with the EMR and telemedicine equipment vendors. Once agreement and clarification were reached, the team created operating guidelines for the use and maintenance of the system, including laminated information sheets with tech support contact numbers to be prominently placed at each of the telemedicine sites.

DID YOU NOTICE

1. Implementing telemedicine and an EMR at the same time can be trouble 1 + 1 = 3. Someone must be on point full time to lead the coordination needed.
2. We are not just buying a glitz technology package from the vendor but also the contractual terms and obligations needed to ensure continuous reliable services. Bravo, Northwest!

Northwest Memorial Example: Alter or create operating guidelines for all involved FET

With input from a designated physician from each of the telemedicine specialties, the Telemedicine Coordinator developed a 'Telemedicine Competency Checklist' for physicians and nursing staff 'tele-presenters'. The checklist was developed for use in conjunction with an orientation videoconference with each of the staff providing telemedicine services. The checklist included review of camera placement/angle, audio and video quality, room lighting, verbal instructions to patients, consents, and other critical items for quality telemedicine encounters. Simple instructions for equipment operation and problem solving were developed, including contact numbers for technical support. These instructions were laminated and placed with each telemedicine camera.

1. Did you notice all the well-thought-out details in the case above?
2. It does not get any better than that!

Medi-Tel's Example: Alter or create operating guidelines for all involved FET

Medi-Tel's IT Director drafted a user manual directed to the 'end user' at the distant care site. The first order of business was a laminated sheet tethered to the telemedicine cart with simple instructions for turning on all of the equipment, operating the remote control, and for contacting technical support. A three ring binder was assembled that included detailed instructions for the videoconference camera and peripheral devices, based on manufacturer-provided materials. Once assembled, the manual was sent to the nurses who provided the field-testing of the equipment for their input. They were instructed to take a red pen to the manual and make candid suggestions for improvement wherever they saw unclear or overly complicated instructions.

DID YOU NOTICE

1. Did they say a three-ring binder and a red pen? Are there no computer-based instructions?
2. Keep instructions simple. A three ring binder will do quite nicely, thank you.

Requirement 3E: Eliminate old FET and operating guidelines

> *Mind-Clearing Example – Imagine a Lighting Director who instructs her technicians to leave the "lighting level marks" from the last production taped on the lighting panels, mixed in with the level marks for the new play.*
>
> *Or imagine a Stage Manager who leaves all of the props from the last play in the same prop racks along with the new props for the new play.*

The bottom line for this FET requirement is simple to say but more difficult to follow: we must get equipment we no longer want to use out of the organization. The undesired FET must be destroyed or put where people can't get their hands on it … or it will be used!

The bottom line for operating guidelines is equally simple but much harder to follow. Essentially we want to have operating guidelines that are no longer relevant, needed, or correct taken out of use in the organization. This simple task is made complex by the fact that many of the operating guidelines that are being used at any one point in time are not written down. It is always tough to get a written policy, procedure, or guideline out of play. It is especially difficult to take unwritten guidelines out of play! But it can be done. The steps we recommend are as follows:

1. Identify the FET operating guidelines that need to be eliminated
2. Create a written draft of any unwanted guidelines that have not been written down (create the draft from what is already written along with information from folks who know the unwritten rules)
3. Get everybody a copy of the "now written" unwanted guidelines
4. Call their attention to the now-written version
5. Tell everybody that those operating guidelines will no longer be used
6. Take the copies away from them, and
7. Destroy the copies letting everybody see you do the destruction!

The commercial airline pilots we discussed in Chapter Five not only systematically deal with changes in work processes and procedures; they also deal with changes in the operating guidelines for the equipment on the aircraft they fly on a daily basis. Not only do pilots systematically remove all old operating guidelines from their flight reference guides, but they systematically examine the cockpits of the aircraft to ensure that there are no lingering operating guidelines present. They have learned that following an old operating guide can really blow up in their faces!

Northwest Memorial Example:
Eliminate FET and operating guidelines

Existing guidelines for coordination of psychiatric emergencies with the Mobile Crisis Team placed in the Emergency Departments of each of the hospitals were removed and replaced with revised guidelines that incorporated the potential access by telemedicine to Mobile Crisis Team staff and the psychiatrist on call.

DID YOU NOTICE ?

1. Is that all there is to it?
2. Yes, and it is critical!

And in conclusion ...

Our task in this chapter has been to focus on the third requirement for transitioning an organization: the physical alteration of the organization's FET. Every organizational change is likely to require new or altered FET to enable the altered work processes designed to fulfill the vision. Regardless of the kind of organizational change or the stimulus for organizational change, we work with the assumption that FET alterations will be required ... unless proven otherwise.

Just as process steps and procedures go together, FET and operating guidelines go together. These guidelines are the written instructions for proper use and operation of FET, be it a ladder, a piece of earth moving equipment or new software. Failing to provide proper operating guidelines for new or altered FET is akin to expecting a new look from a play that is opening with the old set and old costumes from the last play.

ROBERT CUYLER, PHD AND DUTCH HOLLAND, PHD

CHAPTER FIVE

Alter Performance Management

> *Mind-Clearing Example – Imagine the Director who talks to the theater company about the new play but fails to put any of the actors under contract for their involvement in the new play.*
>
> *Imagine that every time the actors try to get closure on what their individual roles will be, the Director says, "Just hang on, I'm sure we'll be able to work something out as we go along."*

THEATER PROFESSIONALS KNOW that no play lasts forever. They also know that transitioning to a new play is the only way they can stay employed. The key mechanism used to transition actors from one play to the next is the "contract" that formalizes the agreement between actor and the theater company to work together, under certain terms, in the next play. Failing to alter the performance management system while expecting successful organizational change is akin to expecting the performance of a new play from actors who are still under exclusive contract for performing the old play!

For successful organization change, there must be physical alteration of the business system that the organization uses to direct and reinforce the performance of its managers and employees. This performance management system is the organization's mechanism for procuring, directing, and retaining the kind of performance it needs. This performance management system must be altered in order to (1) reinforce the transition to the new organizational future and (2) to dis-incentivize failure to transition to the new future

For successful organizational change, employees must be "under contract" or "under agreement" to perform their:

- **New roles** after changeover to the new way of doing business (e.g., agreeing to perform in a new nursing position, to become the operator of new equipment, to head a newly-created department, etc.)

In addition, all employees must be under agreement to perform during the organization's transition to the new way of doing business during which they will perform their:

- **Current roles**, (their "day job" of lab work, nursing, completing the October financials, etc.)

- **Transition work or change work** (attending training, helping to re-write procedures, testing and calibrating new equipment, etc.)

This performance break-out looks good, doesn't it? But getting these roles all sorted out is easier said than done.

> *Very Important Note to the Reader!! Detour starts here!!*
>
> *As the title of this chapter says, our primary focus will be on managing the transition of employees from one way of doing business to another.*
>
> *HOWEVER, we have learned the hard way that most of us carry a set of assumptions about managing employees that are just plain destructive to organizational change.*
>
> *On the other hand, most of us have our heads straight about contractors. Therefore, we will take a detour and talk about how we manage contractors or vendors first in order to convey what we see as the "right mindset" to use with employees as we transition them from one way of doing business to another.*

After nearly forty years of consulting work with organizations that were trying to change, we can categorically state that the biggest obstacle to successful organizational change we have seen is the way managers handle "work agreements" in the organization. While altering the organization's physical FET seems to be the best-done part of organizational change, altering the performance management system of the organization seems to be the most difficult by far.

ROBERT CUYLER, PHD AND DUTCH HOLLAND, PHD

Every organization has a performance management system of some kind whether it is formal and explicit or informal and not written down. There are two classic performance management systems that organizations use to steer the performance of the people they employ. The first system, (the Detour we mentioned in the box above) frequently called contractor management, is used for steering the performance of those workers whom the company considers as outside contractors or vendors.

The second mechanism, the employee performance management system, is used for steering the performance of those persons whom the organization considers as full or part-time employees. Interestingly enough, theatre companies will frequently use both: contractor management for actors and an employee performance management system for everyone else. As we said earlier, our focus in this chapter is primarily on employee management systems, but please allow us to detour and cover contractor performance first.

Managing contractor performance: the Detour begins!

Most organization members are generally familiar with the way contractors will be managed (after all, most everybody has engaged a "contractor" to mow their lawn, put down new flooring in the kitchen, or complete their tax return). Any contractor management system, including the one we use informally at home, includes such critical and logical steps as follows:

1. Defining the desired work the company wants from a contractor
2. Locating, negotiating, and reaching agreement with a contractor to perform the desired work
3. Explaining the work to be done to the contractor and ensuring understanding
4. Familiarizing the contractor with the way the company works
5. Authorizing the contractor to begin work
6. Monitoring the contractor's performance over time
7. Ensuring that the contractor has completed the required work and
8. Ensuring the contractor is paid in accordance with the negotiated agreement.

The primary administrative vehicle used in contractor management is the written contract. This instrument, signed by both the contractor and a representative of the organization, contains key sections that are necessary to ensure the agreement is carried out with integrity: the contractor completes the defined work for the organization … and the organization provides agreed-to compensation for the work done.

Expect to see the following key sections in a "contractor's contract:"

- Statement of Work – identifies precisely what the contractor is to do for the organization during the specified time period of the contract
- Qualifications – specifies what skills and capabilities the contractor is required to bring to the assignment
- Performance Evaluation – tells the contractor how performance will be monitored, measured, and evaluated
- Payment – spells out the agreed-to payment terms and conditions for the contract work
- General Terms – describes how the contractor and organization will do business together during the contract period, including how disputes will be handled.

Contracting for vendor performance is normally handled by the organization's procurement function or Human Resources department. The day-to-day management of the vendor is usually handled by an operating manager who is employing the vendor's services in designated work (i.e., the accounting department head manages the work of a contract accountant). This employing manager directs the vendor's day-to-day performance as necessary within the scope and arrangements of the contract.

As the work needs of the organization change, the employing manager works with the contracting officer and the vendor to modify and re-negotiate the vendor contract. The employing manager works in this fashion, keeping the vendor and the contract aligned with the work requirements of the organization ... until there is no longer a need for the services of the contractor. At completion of the agreed-to work, the contract is terminated, and the contractor and the organization go their separate ways to work together again in the future ... or to never work together again.

End of Detour!

From this point we are back on track to cover the focus of this chapter: Altering Performance Management for Employees. Hopefully we have conveyed two important aspects of organizational change management:

ROBERT CUYLER, PHD AND DUTCH HOLLAND, PHD

> - *It is critical to use the contractor-management mindset when managing employee performance, and*
> - *Today's organization workforce has fewer employees and more contractors or vendors, so vendor management is more than an educational tool ... it is a requirement for organizational change today.*

Managing employee performance

In theory, employee performance is managed very much like contractor performance. An employee must be "under agreement" to do the work of the organization in order to receive the rewards for work. When we use the term "contract" with employees, we are usually not talking about a written contract like that used with vendors. In practice, very few employees have formal written contracts but they are "under agreement" with the organization.

The point is that all employees work under an agreement with the company (the equivalent of a contract): employees agree that they are to do certain things for the organization in order to be paid. The company agrees to pay x amount for y work, while the employee agrees to do y work for x amount.

The steps we take to get employees under agreement and to work for the company are similar to the steps we take with contractors. We must systematically and responsibly take the following interrelated steps when we manage employee performance:

1. Think through what work we want an employee to do.
2. Find (or have Human Resources find) an employee who has the skills, capabilities, and initiative necessary to do that work.
3. Communicate the specific work to the employee and secure her understanding and willingness to do the work.
4. Formalize the agreement to work together with proper hiring paperwork and a handshake and "welcome aboard speech."
5. Provide any final training needed by the employee to be able to do the work.
6. Have the employee begin work ... including taking personal initiative to perform to the needed level.
7. Ensure the employee gets feedback on how her work is progressing.

8. Evaluate employee performance and ensure the employee is properly/fairly paid for their services under the hiring agreement.

Our key message is a simple one: for long-term success in employee performance management, employees must always stay under agreement to do the work of the company. And as the requirements of the work change, it is up to the employing manager to keep an up-to-date agreement with employees in effect at all times.

> For example, let's say that an employee has been under agreement to do tasks "A through F" in a company department. Let's say that the work needed in that department changes, for whatever reason. It is up to the employing manager to get the employee under agreement to do the new work – say, tasks "B through H." The employing manager follows the steps shown above – from understanding the new work, through communicating the new work to the employee; gaining his understanding and agreement to start two new tasks, stop doing one old task and to continue doing the remainder of the old tasks; providing training as needed for the new tasks; starting the new employee to work on the new tasks; providing feedback to the employee on performance; and ensuring that the employee's performance is fully evaluated at the end of the year and that the employee is properly paid for doing the new job and not the old one.

As in the case of vendor management, the employing manager works with representatives of the Human Resources department for assistance in completing the basic steps in managing employee performance. While the details may vary from company to company, it is critical for the employing managers and the human resource managers to come to their own clear agreement on how they will work together to ensure effective and efficient performance management.

When the work needed from the employee changes, the supervisor explains the employee's job and the change to be made. The manager and the employee come to agreement that the employee will perform the modified job. While there is no written contract to change, there is a company job description to be altered (if the new work is not covered under the current description's scope).

The employee may need training for the changed job, and if so, the manager needs to make arrangements. The employee performs the changed job until the job is changed again (and it will change again because no way of doing business lasts forever). At the end of the designated performance period, the worker's job performance in the modified job is formally evaluated and the results are discussed with the employee. The results of the performance appraisal then become input to the company's compensation system that ultimately determines employee compensation.

At this point the similarity of vendor performance management and employee management is clear. The description of employee performance is clean and crisp in our treatment here. In the real world of work, however, the process will become blurred and fuzzy unless the appropriate manager exerts strong control of the process.

Identify and dispel deadly assumptions about performance management transition

The step of transitioning the performance management system to enable an organization to move to a new way of doing business is among the most challenging tasks that managers face in change. Why most challenging? It seems simple enough. Because this assumption is one that managers want to make since they see it as making their jobs easier and less stressful.

From a mechanical point of view, altering performance management is relatively simple, but from an interpersonal point of view, it is one of the most dreaded tasks that many managers must take on. Most managers do not look forward to talking to their direct reports about new standards of performance, about changes in the way performance will be evaluated, or about changing compensation patterns or arrangements.

Consequently this assumption allows managers to dodge the real truth that must be conveyed to employees in an organizational change: "We are making a change, your job will be different, your evaluation will be done against your new job, not the old one, and your compensation will be directly linked to your level of performance in the new way of doing business."

Step	Change-Blocking Assumptions	Disabling Behavior by Management	Proven Consequences
Requirement Four: Transitioning the Performance Management System	Changing their work will • be hurtful for employees and • unpleasant for me. "After all, this change is about their work, not what we pay."	• Talking about change without connecting change to employee evaluation and compensation • Failure to alter either job descriptions or compensation payoffs • Failure to be proactive about performance short-falls or failures	• Unwillingness to change • Lowered Morale

Hearing the suggestion to "leave the employees alone; we don't need to talk to them about pay; that's a hot subject and they will all get on board as we go along" gives away the presence of deadly assumptions and calls for the change leader to dispel them in any way possible, starting with the proven consequences in the table above.

Take these action steps to transition performance management

Failure to alter performance management will literally stop an organizational change in its tracks. Take the following five steps to transition performance management:

Action steps to transition performance management

- 4A: Identify and alter individual roles
- 4B: Complete one-on-one contracting with all affected employees
- 4C: Train all employees in the new roles they will play
- 4D: Identify and alter the system for evaluating performance
- 4E: Alter and communicate communication payoffs

Requirement 4A: Identify and alter individual roles and goals needed for change

Mind-Clearing Example – Imagine a Director who can't decide how many dancers will be in the chorus line for his new musical. Imagine the Director responded to one of the dancers: "I don't know if you will be in the line or not. Just work your way in somewhere and we'll see what develops!"

ROBERT CUYLER, PHD AND DUTCH HOLLAND, PHD

Or imagine a Director who has decided she wants a certain actor in the new production but who is unwilling to decide which of three roles might be the best use of the actor's talent!

We use an organization's performance management system to both guide employee performance and then to ensure the employee is paid for his performance. This step in engineering the performance management system is all about identifying the specific roles and goals that workers will need to develop and play after an organizational change. Just as each actor in a play must have a role, so must each and every employee. We define "role" as an organization member's job, his assigned set of tasks and responsibilities. (From our earlier discussion of performance management, an employee's role is his agreed-to statement of work that he is paid to accomplish.)

In addition to role descriptions, workers need specific targets or goals for designated time periods. We want to set specific goals and objectives for individual and team performance to meet the needs of the process objectives already set in Requirement Two: Altering Work Processes. We want to have specific measures that can be monitored by both workers and managers to understand and manage the level of worker performance in his new role after the change.

Change requires new or altered roles and goals

The job for the change leader is first and foremost to identify what roles will be needed to fulfill the change vision. He then must identify the goals that need to be associated with each role to meet the level of performance expected in the new way of doing business. Then the change leader must identify which new roles will be needed (with accompanying goals), which existing roles will need to change (the direction of those changes), and what roles will not change ... and then to communicate that information personally to everybody in the organization. Now this sounds simple ... and it is. But it can become a big job since some organizations have many managers and employees to get into new roles or to "steady" in old roles.

Regardless of the kind of organizational change or the stimulus for organizational change, new roles and goals or alterations of some existing roles and goals will be required.

- If an organization decides to **change its business strategy** to become the most reliable service provider, for example, many, if not all, of the organization's work processes will need to change to take out waste and risk-prone, non-standard steps or to alter the sequence of steps, and so on. In addition, the company's marketing processes would need to be altered to add promotional steps and materials that stress changed features and outcome measures of the organization's service delivery. This kind of strategy change will require that people do things differently (i.e., have their roles and goals altered) in accordance with the new work processes.

- If an organization decides to **change one of the technologies** that it uses in its business, role and goal alterations are almost certain to be involved. Work steps to set-up the new FET and to use the output of the new system will need to be assigned to somebody (i.e., become a part of his roles in the company). A new software tool, for instance, will likely require either new data elements to enter the software and/or new steps to use the output of the software requiring alteration of the roles and goals of the assigned workers.

- If an organization decides to make **a change in its culture**, several process changes will result as organization members begin to approach the job differently. If, for example, the desired cultural change is to become more attentive to customers, changes will probably need to be made in the steps used in the design of customer service into the work processes, behavior styles and feedback systems … impacting the roles and goals of the organization members assigned to those Departments. We believe that the primary tool for changing an organization's culture is the performance management system. Culture change begins with the revision of employee roles to include the desired behaviors wanted in the new culture followed by compensation rules that pay off for workers using the desired behaviors.

- If an organization decides to make **a change in its organizational structure**, alterations will likely be required both in management/decision-making processes as well as in the work processes performed by members of the units that are involved. These process alterations will result in role alterations for managers and workers alike. (Note: In almost forty years of consulting, we have seen companies make many changes to their organization structures that were entirely

ROBERT CUYLER, PHD AND DUTCH HOLLAND, PHD

superficial in nature, leading to no substantial changes to the four mechanical attributes emphasized in this book. To us, an organization change should be focused on bringing better resourcing ... of people and skills ... to bear on substantial changes to work processes. In short, we tell our clients to forget about changing the organizational structure if they do not intend to make work processes more effective or efficient.)

This first step in transitioning the organization's performance management system is to identify a role and goal for everybody in the new way of doing business. Everyone must have an identified role and goal for performance after the organization does its change. For many organizational changes, the roles and goals of some employees will remain unchanged.

Use a team to identify new and altered organizational roles and goals

We want to finish this step with five end products:

1. a list of the new roles that will be needed,
2. a list of current roles that will need to be altered, along with
3. the direction/nature of the required alterations, and
4. a list of the organizational roles that will not need to be altered to enact the vision.
5. a list of notes that will no longer be needed.

We generate these lists from analysis of four resources:

- List of work processes to be altered
- List of FET to be altered
- The organization chart and accompanying tables, and
- The organization's master listing of personnel.

The first step in identifying needed role and goal alterations (and/or new roles) is to systematically go through the organization's work processes and FET to visualize any modifications that will be needed in roles and goals for organization members. In previous steps ... alteration of work processes (Chapter Three) and alteration of FET (Chapter Four) ... we generated lists entitled: "process alterations needed to reach the vision" and "FET alterations needed to reach the vision." These lists are the obvious starting places for identifying role and goal alterations or new roles.

Support workers as they develop needed roles and goals

> *Mind-Clearing Example – Imagine an actor who has just signed a contract for a role in a new play. Imagine that actor reading the script to better understand his role and then waiting for the director to come around and tell him exactly how to play each detail of the part.*
>
> *When asked about his approach, the actor says, "Hey, I just go on stage and do what I have been told to do."*

Organizations should expect that workers will take the needed initiative to develop their new or altered roles ... when cued by their bosses to do so. A boss must make it a given that her workers will exercise the personal leadership needed to develop (fill out the details) of the new roles needed in the new way of doing business. Fortunately most employees will take that initiative and work out their own details.

Experience has taught us that change leaders need to orchestrate the role development process to ensure that all workers get their needed role and goal alterations identified and made. Failure to use a firm hand to ensure that such work gets done will inevitably produce great variance in scheduled completion of the alterations (many workers will be late if left to their own devices) as well as great variation in the thoroughness and level of detail of role descriptions and documentation.

An approach that has worked for us for years is as simple as this: we encourage old pro employees to develop their own needed roles and goals alterations with little assistance from the boss. On the other hand, we recommend that the boss take the lead in developing the roles and goals of rookie employees who are new to the work of the company. Regardless of who works through the alterations, those alterations still need to be done on schedule for the change to happen as expected.

In the end, it is each individual worker who will have to work through the details of his role and goals in order to meet the expectations of the organization after the change. But change leaders do need to take firm control of the process of identifying and ensuring role and goal alterations to have any real chance to have the organizational change ... on target, on time, and on budget.

ROBERT CUYLER, PHD AND DUTCH HOLLAND, PHD

Northwest Memorial Example:
Workers develop roles and goals

As a part of the EMR roll-out, one physician came forward and said he would like to try his hand at leading the medical staff review of clinical templates that would be used in the surgical, cardiology and psychiatry initiatives. Existing paper templates were sent to the physicians involved in the telemedicine project for their input on modifications to existing protocols and their translation to electronic format. This particular MD had been an IT fan for years and was especially skillful at both IT and in getting others involved in working out how the EMR system would work and how individual jobs would need to be modified for both IT staff and for the clinicians who would use the systems on a daily basis.

DID YOU NOTICE

1. Did we talk before about the importance of telemedicine business experience on the implementation project?
2. If we did, it bears repeating!

Medi-Tel Example:
Workers develop roles and goals

As telemedicine represented a new role for all of the physicians except for Dr. Janssen, some significant shifts in practice were anticipated, not the least of which was the reality of being 'on camera'. The concept of 'stage presence' was unfamiliar and a little off-putting to several of the doctors. Dr. Janssen prevailed on his colleagues to record their initial consultations with the logistical support cases to see for themselves how they presented on camera. Several were quite chagrinned to see themselves as a patient would.

Until viewing themselves, they were not fully aware of the impact of how they introduced themselves, their eye contact (or lack thereof), and other 'stage presence' variables on the quality of their interactions with patients. With this experience vividly in mind, each doctor agreed that their telemedicine presentation skills would be assessed via a 'telemedicine competency checklist' and that any new doctors joining the physician pool would be similarly briefed and assessed before going live as a Medi-Tel doctor.

The doctors' own experience led to considerable discussion around the reality of working with customer organizations with employees that Medi-Tel did not employ but who would be key players in the delivery of telemedicine. The group suddenly became aware of the tensions between a) wanting to find business rapidly for the company and accommodating as necessary to meet their growth goals and b) requiring the customer to conform to some fairly stringent requirements on their in end in order to become a customer. Steve Ames drafted some additional covenants detailing the obligations of the customer and passed them along to Medi-Tel's attorney to add to Medi-Tel's template contract.

DID YOU NOTICE

1. Developing roles and goals is a contact sport.
2. Role development and self-awareness go hand in hand.
3. Role development only works if each of the telemedicine players takes personal responsibility.
4. When working with others whose cooperation you need but who you don't directly supervise, walk softly and carry a big grin!

Document the new and altered roles and goals

Companies vary in the ways they handle the contents of roles of organization members. Some companies have written roles and goals for their positions and some do not. While there is great variation among companies, the most popular device for recording the contents of roles is the job description with an accompanying annual goals list. Our bottom line is simple, we don't really care what kind of device the company uses to document roles. We just recommend that there be such a device, and that it be used systematically. The written job description with accompanying goals for the new and altered roles is the equivalent of the new statement of work that will be expected from vendors or employees after the change over to the new way of doing business.

ROBERT CUYLER, PHD AND DUTCH HOLLAND, PHD

Determine the compensation level for new and altered roles

The last critical part of the role alteration step is to determine the compensation level that matches the new and altered roles needed for the Vision. It will do no good to offer an employee an altered role if the offered compensation is not enough to get the employee to accept it. This critical step to determine compensation must be initiated by the change leader assisted by a representative from Human Resources. That HR representative must ensure that the altered roles and the determined compensation for those roles fit with the company's normal Human Resources Compensation policy and procedures (which normally include benchmarking pay in the local job market):

- **No compensation change for typical role alteration:** If the altered role still fits within the same job classification (and labor market), the organization should not need to change compensation for the role. In fact, one of our key goals in identifying needed role alterations is to keep jobs within the same families and classification ranges.

- **No pay for routine change:** An organization cannot give extra compensation, a raise or a bonus, for every change an organization might make in the way it does business. If a company were forced to pay everyone an extra amount for every change, that company would soon find itself with a cost structure that would be out of line with the market place. A key idea is that once organizations and individuals have mastered change, they will both be willing and able to make normal changes without a great deal of support, attention, and without feeling that extra compensation is due.

- **Pay for role alterations that significantly change the employment situation:** Occasionally, when organizations alter jobs so that more or higher skills are involved in the new work, it may be necessary to adjust the employee's compensation package. Some companies, for example, have procedures for grading jobs on difficulty, the level of accountability for results, the number of people supervised, etc. If role alterations move an employee to a new salary classification level, the company will need to be prepared to pay for it.

Northwest Memorial Example:
Identify and alter individual roles and goals

From the beginning of the Telemedicine project, a Human Resources specialist had been assigned to work with the design team to be on the lookout for the need for role and goal changes. As changes areas were identified and new roles developed, she produced a draft of the altered job descriptions for nursing staff who would 'tele-present' in cardiology and surgery. When it was clear that roles were fully designed, the HR specialist ensured that all bases were touched to get formal jobs descriptions in place.

DID YOU NOTICE

1. Job descriptions are like contracts, and Northwest worked to get descriptions in place. This may not be glamorous work, and it may not be fun for you, but going without them will be trouble ... sooner than later.
2. Use the Human Resources specialists, and let them do their jobs. Yes, they are usually not very flexible in letting you do whatever you want with workers and their job descriptions.
3. HR specialists know how to do it right and how to keep you out of the courtroom or jail house!

Medi-Tel Example:
Identify and alter individual roles and goals

Physicians were unused to the concept of working under the structure of a job description. Frequent reminders that Medi-Tel was a start-up company and not a conventional medical practice were necessary to nudge the doctors into accepting this new structure. While comfortable with measures of clinical quality, the doctors had to make adjustments to take responsibility for customer service and productivity, not only for patient care but also for new business development.

Realizing that Medi-Tel would be hugely dependent on effective communication, medical record transfer, scheduling, and patient presentation at the distant site, the organization reached out to the Human Resource Director of the multi-specialty clinic to draft a model job description for the tele-presenters and coordinators that worked for customers. Having been involved in several healthcare start-ups, Mr. Ames warned that their fledgling enterprise could unravel unless Medi-Tel exerted significant control over the roles, actions, and responsibilities of their customers' critical personnel.

ROBERT CUYLER, PHD AND DUTCH HOLLAND, PHD

1. It is OK to write job descriptions for the professionals in your partner institutions.
2. Just make sure to do three things:
   a. Lead with your organization's job descriptions.
   b. Put the words "Draft" and "For Discussion Only" on top of their job descriptions.
   c. Walk softly and carry a big grin!

Requirement 4B: Complete one-on-one contracting with every affected worker

> *Mind-Clearing Example – Imagine a Director who is ready to begin rehearsals for a new play but who has not put any of the actors under contract for the play.*
>
> *Imagine the Director getting feedback that the actors wanted their contracts signed ... but who stated, "Tell them not to worry ... I've always been a man of my word!"*

When an organization changes, some people will have different jobs. Jobs may be anything from almost the same as before the change to radically different. When we want workers to do that different job, we must put them under agreement to do so. And when we need other workers to keep doing their old jobs into the new organization, we need to confirm their agreement to do so. To make things more difficult, we must get folks into new agreements and confirming old agreement on a one-on-one basis.

Workers in an existing organization are usually under agreement to do current work. Until that agreement is changed with them, workers will consciously or unconsciously tend to keep doing what they have been doing. Not only do we need to get workers under agreement for the new job, but we must get them to agree to continue the old job until the moment of change-over to the new one. This step in transitioning the performance management system is all about getting a new agreement in place with the workers involved in an organizational change so that they will be willing to perform to expectations. And unlike many other steps in organizational change, the change leader cannot do this step. Only the employee's immediate supervisor can get an employee under a new agreement.

Implementation of the new way of doing business cannot occur until each employee is prepared and under agreement for the performance needed. Terms of the agreement call on each employee to use the altered processes and FET to meet the goals and objectives associated with their position. Getting workers under agreement takes careful preparation, systematic execution of one or more one-on-one contracting sessions, and after-session follow-up to ensure the agreement is sound and can be managed.

Get clear on the agreement that is needed between the organization and the employee

Before meeting with workers on a one-on-one basis, it is critical for the boss to get clear on what he will be trying to accomplish. When this step is completed, we want each worker under agreement to:

- Play a new or modified role in the organization after the change goes into effect (i.e., to act the altered role and meet specific goals in the new way of doing business)

- Continue to perform at the needed level in the current job until time to formally change to the new way of doing business

- Do those Change Work transition tasks as required to make all the needed mechanical changes to get to the new role (i.e., help in defining the new role and goals, participating in training and work process walk-throughs, etc.)

- Accept the compensation package and job title that will be offered (either changed or unchanged from the present organization)

Get ready for the contracting session

A boss cannot get a worker under a new agreement unless he is under such a new agreement himself! Imagine a Director trying to get actors under contract for a new play when the Director is not sure she has a job! Getting bosses on board first means that contracting will need to be done in an organizational cascade … from the top of the units affected by the change to the bottom.

The boss must also be ready to explain the vision, the work process and FET alterations that will be needed for that change … and consequently, the role and goal alterations required. Readiness also includes enthusiasm and high expectations for the organizational change. Regardless of the enthusiasm, optimism, and hopes of the change leader in the organization, it is the boss's expectations for the future that count with the employee in the contracting session. Bosses who cannot muster enthusiasm for such sessions with their employees are clearly not under agreement themselves. It is up to each boss to get ready, be ready ... or go back to her boss and re-contract!

In addition to organizational direction, the boss should be prepared to offer and discuss a fair compensation package that

- the worker is likely to accept and
- the company is able to afford.

The supervisor should have checked with both the change leader and the organization's Human Resources Department to get clear on the compensation package to be offered and whether or not there is negotiating room on any parts of the package.

The materials the boss will need to have in hand for the one-on-one session with each employee includes the following:

- The relevant role or job description and job title as it will apply under the new way of doing business (frequently the title will be unchanged)
- A statement of individual goals associated with the new way of doing business
- The organization chart as it will look under the new way of doing business
- Any team assignments relevant to the new job
- The offered compensation package, and
- The effective date for the organization change and any changes in compensation

The last and one of the most critical parts of the preparation will be to schedule the worker for the one-on-one session. Schedule a meeting place that will be private during your conversation with the worker, a conversation that could last from 30 minutes to an hour. Be sure to tell the worker that the purpose of the session is to formally invite the worker to be a part of the upcoming organizational change. The worker should have heard about the change multiple times ... if we have executed our communication plans as outlined in Requirement One: Communicating Vision.

Conduct the contracting session to get agreements in place

The contracting meeting is a business meeting, and it needs to have a planned business agenda. The contracting meeting may go as smooth as silk with the employee readily agreeing and getting on board (such is usually the case in organizations that have mastered change). Frequently, however, the process does not go straight through in a 30 minute meeting. The boss may encounter one of the following situations, particularly if the organizational change will be perceived as a major one by the employee.

- **The employee needs time to consider:** If that is the case, agree to meet again with the employee after two or three days. Some employees need the time to consider, or they want to check with a spouse. They may even want to get the reaction of other employees who are going through contracting sessions.

- **The employee wants to negotiate:** We are offering, in essence, a different job to the employee. Negotiation should not be a surprise and might be looked on as a normal part of a business transaction. The employee needs to be able to consider the new job along with the offered compensation. The boss must be able to handle the negotiation based on his preparation for the meeting.

- **The employee is unwilling to take the offer:** Some employees may not be willing to take on a new or different role for their own reasons (e.g., the new position calls for a move or the employee's retirement is very near). If so, the boss might want to be respectful of that decision and do what he can to begin to transition the employee out of the current position and into a new place in the organization before the effective time of organizational change.

  Having an employee say, "No, thank you," in a contracting session is not necessarily bad news. If this employee would not have been cooperative in the organizational change, it is better by far that we find out about that in the contracting session and not in the first few weeks of the change when the employee's lack of cooperation could hurt the organization's performance.

- **The Employee is not sure:** Some employees may not be sure whether or not they want to move to an altered position. Some employees may not be

ROBERT CUYLER, PHD AND DUTCH HOLLAND, PHD

able to get rid of their uncertainty until after they are in the altered role. All this is understandable and acceptable, to a point. The supervisor should not entertain the idea of letting the employee try the new role without getting the employee to agree to a "100% effort" to do the new role as it needs to be done for a trial period. This agreement to play at 100% is necessary to

- ensure that the organization can count on the needed performance from that role and so that

- the employee will really understand and appreciate what the altered role requires ... and can, therefore, make a better decision about taking the position long-term.

Over the years we have had several managers balk at the contracting idea because, as they said, "You are serving up this organizational change as a take-it or leave-it situation!" Our standard response has become: "Yes, in a way, it is a take-it or leave-it situation. The organization's leadership has decided to make the change. The needed work process alterations and FET alterations have been made and the role is fixed." The supervisor can then either sign the employee to the role or assist the employee in finding other work.

The only thing that is optional is whether or not the current employee chooses to work in the new way of doing business." As one manager puts it, "This is what our work family is now doing! Do you want to continue to be a part of our family?" Imagine a contracting session between a Director and an actor. When the actor is offered a role in the new play, he says, "No thank you, I like the old play better, and I'll just stick with my part in that play!" A fly on the wall might say, "What play? Hello, the old play has left the building."

Seal the contracting session with a handshake

We shake hands when we buy something. We shake hands when we sell something. We shake hands after a job is offered and accepted. And we shake hands after we have agreement with the employee to move to a new way of doing business. "Let's shake on our new business deal!"

Most companies do not do a good job of changing the agreement with the employee on a one-on-one basis. Companies try to change employee agreements in batch with several employees in the same room listening to a big boss explain what the company needs "from each and every one of you!" That's an important speech to make, and I wouldn't do away with it, but I would make sure that the speech is followed by a one-on-one meeting between every affected employee and his boss. In that meeting it is up to the boss, representing the employer, to ensure that the employee understands the need from him/her to do the job differently. And it's up to the boss to look into the employee's eyes and confirm agreement to do it the new way … and then to consummate the deal with our culture's symbol of agreement – the handshake!

The handshake is the very last act we use to get managers and employees to change to the new direction in the company. The handshake finalizes the re-negotiation of an employee's role in the new future of the organization. The handshake represents the employee's intention to perform to the new role, as he or she understands it … for the accepted compensation package. The handshake represents the company's (and management's) intention to expect and support performance of the new role. Last but not least, the handshake cancels the old role agreement between company and employee when the change-over to the new way of doing business occurs.

The handshake, completed under an eyeball-to-eyeball gaze, signals two people's intention to go forward together toward a new way of working. And if either party cannot execute the handshake, everybody knows where they are … and they then can solve the problem of lack of agreement – either through more explanation, negotiation, or by transfer or by terminating the relationship.

Record the new agreement

Take that last step and document the organization's records to show that the employee accepted the altered role at the offered or negotiated compensation level. The record should also note whether the acceptance by the employee is for some trial period or for the long term. We also recommend that for major organizational changes, the boss pen a letter to the employee thanking him for accepting the altered role in the new organization. Many managers have wished they had such a letter after an employee disavowed any knowledge of the impending change and/or the contracting session with the boss.

Northwest Memorial Example: Complete One-on-One Contracting for Every Affected Person

The Chief Strategy Officer started this step by having one-on-one meetings with each of the physician section chiefs and visits to each of the four rural hospitals for meetings with the chief nursing officer and nurse managers involved in the telemedicine project, ensuring their readiness to assume their role in the Telemedicine project and asking for their commitment to the System initiative, its directions and goals.

When each of the direct reports shook hands with the boss, he requested that each of them repeat the exercise with direct reports. Generally this was done, but some direct reports were slow to find the time to have the one-on-one meetings. Fortunately, the end of the year was approaching, and the required performance appraisal meetings provided the opportunity for the handshake.

DID YOU NOTICE

1. Ask for commitment to the impending change to telemedicine. There is nothing wrong with that simple business question.
2. If a worker cannot commit, then the issue must be worked then and there.
3. It is certainly OK for a worker to say that they don't want to commit to a new role.
4. At that point things are certain, however:
    a. The worker does not have permission to stay in their current role and continue to work the old way (i.e., without telemedicine)
    b. When it is time for the telemedicine practice to go live, the role being discussed must be occupied by a worker committed to the new way of doing business.
5. The handshake is very valuable to "seal the deal" with the worker. Try it, you'll like it!

Medi-Tel Example: Complete One-on-One Contracting for Every Affected Person

One-to-one contracting within Medi-Tel was relatively easy among the doctors. Dr. Janssen paid particular attention to Dr. Post's early misgivings about the changes in roles and expectations that would be involved for the Medi-Tel physician team. As the company neared formal launch, Dr. Post struggled less with the transitions to medical entrepreneurship and could enthusiastically get on board with his colleagues. Steve Ames and Dr. Jannsen tracked down each of the personnel who would provide support roles from the multi-specialty practice (IT, Human Resources, Scheduling) and personally invited, thanked, and enlisted them for their work with Medi-Tel.

The CEO and COO also realized that the same approach would be vital as they launched collaboration with each of their customer organizations, now and in the future. In the orientation process, Medi-Tel's leadership would communicate the vision of their telemedicine practice and invite their customers to their joint endeavor, followed by acceptance and a handshake.

DID YOU NOTICE

1. Notice that this contracting was done by the boss, having the commitment conversation with each physician to be involved in the telemedicine practice.
2. The vision, invitation, acceptance, handshake meeting was one of many that these same people had had together. Only after the team is leaning in the desired direction, should the change leader go for the summary conversation and the handshake.

Requirement 4C: Train all employees in their new roles

> *Mind-Clearing Example – Imagine a Director who doesn't think the theater company can spare the time for rehearsals.*
>
> *Or imagine the Director who says, "All the members of my company are experienced stage professionals ... they certainly don't need to go through the humiliation of rehearsing a play in front of their peers and an empty theater!"*

When workers start doing work that is relatively new to them, they need to know what they are doing. How is that for a revolutionary idea? If workers are asked to change to work that they do not know how to do, they will not be able to perform well, and they will probably have bad feelings of fear, uncertainty, and doubt. This step in altering the performance management system is all about getting the necessary training to workers involved in an organizational change so that they will be able to perform to expectations – theirs and the company's.

Many managers seem to think that training employees for organizational change is no big deal. Actually, we have found a huge amount of confusion around the training that accompanies organizational change. What we want for organization members is the kind of training that theater company members get in their rehearsal for a new play. Employees need training in their roles. Organization members in many of today's organizations have gotten every other kind of training you can think of, without getting any training or rehearsal at all on the roles they are to perform. We have seen the following training courses offered (or made mandatory) for organization members with good intentions of preparing them for an upcoming organizational change:

- The psychological theory of personal change
- Personality types and how they respond to change
- Stress management
- Learning theory
- Creative thinking and innovation
- The Theory of the learning organization

… and we could go on!

All the above course titles may be legitimate areas of study … they just don't fit well with an organization that is trying to move from the way it operates now to a new way that has been designed for the future. To make our point, consider the following:

> *Mind Clearing Example – Imagine a theatrical director announcing the following to her actors readying for the next play: "I have exciting news! Rather than doing those dreary rehearsals we usually do for a new play, I have booked a professor from Columbia to come in-house to teach us the following courses in lieu of rehearsals:*
>
> - *TA 101: History and theory of the theater*
> - *TA 102: Modern musical comedy in the American Theater*

> - *TA 103: The Economics of the Modern Entertainment Business*
> - *TA 104: Psychological profiles of Actors with Stage Fright"*
>
> *How would you like to hear what the actors have to say about that bright idea? Imagine that their continued requests for rehearsals of the script are answered with even more courses like the ones above (from CCNY this time) instead of intensive focus on the task at hand ... learning the ins and outs of the play they will be performing in a matter of weeks!*

Yes, training is important for organizational change, but it must be training that directly contributes and counts toward mastery of the new organizational play that is to be performed!

Get clear on the objectives of training

The objectives for training in the context of organizational change are clear: we want the workers in the organization to be able to competently perform the work that is required for the new way of doing business that is described in our vision. We want the workers to be able to do their newly-assigned roles at the needed performance levels, whether their roles are new to them or alterations of the roles they currently perform. We want to ensure that individuals will have the knowledge, skills, and attitudes needed to perform to altered statements of work

We want the kind of hands-on training that a theater company gets as it goes through its rehearsals for the new production. Just as we want a cast to run through rehearsal after rehearsal leading up to a final "dress rehearsal," we want workers to be trained to needed performance levels in the roles they will play in the new way of doing business.

Arrange and conduct the needed training

We want to arrange for the training needed to raise knowledge, skills, and attitudes to the levels necessary for satisfactory performance after the change. When many managers think about training, they envision classroom training in which workers hear about the new tasks they will need to be able to do in

ROBERT CUYLER, PHD AND DUTCH HOLLAND, PHD

the new way of doing business. While such classroom training is useful for moving the workforce to a level of awareness and preparation for the change, the kind of training that most fills the bill for preparation for organizational change is hands-on, practical training. In practical training, the workers get the opportunity:

- to do actual work
- using the new work processes
- with any new enabling FET
- on a repetitive basis
- until they develop the needed level of proficiency.

The kind of arrangements that organizations need to make to execute training probably needs to vary with the intensity and importance of the organizational change. When proficiency in work processes or FET is required for safety reason or high business consequence reasons, training needs to be intensively applied.

- **High proficiency required:** For critical organizational changes requiring high proficiency of workers as soon as the organizational change goes into effect, training must be systematic, intense, and repetitively delivered. We watched up close and personal both NASA and the US Air Force training its crews to perform a new mission ... and that training was intense, starting months before the new mission commence date and went on daily until all crews had the needed level of proficiency. In such situations, individual crew members received literally hundreds of hours of training before that had the necessary level of proficiency.

- **Minimum proficiency required:** For organizational changes that only require a minimum level of worker proficiency at the time of the change, training can be applied much less intensively. It is still critical, however, that training move the workforce up to that minimum level before we throw the switch at Change Over. We have seen many organizational changes that involved work process changes with altered computer screens. In many of these changes, the change leaders took the step of arranging some computer-use training before the change-over, but then they left the workers to sort out the best use of the software after the change.

- **Learning curve required:** For organizational changes that require a long trip on the learning curve, training must be carefully arranged to get the workforce to the needed level of proficiency within both the schedule and economic constraints of the change. (The learning curve idea has been around since the 1930's and deals with the rate of learning that takes place as workers double the amount of repetition of the job. Industrial engineers can calculate the likely learning rate for the specific operations involved in an organizational change.)

The seriousness of your training program sends a signal to workers about the importance of the change to the organization, and therefore to them

- Use the best trainers, not the folks who are easiest to make available.
- Consider using first line supervisors for training because they will be on point for day-to-day, over-the-shoulder coaching and re-training
- Don't train so far in advance that the workers "forget before they use"
- Keep to the schedule … don't compromise or give up allocated time
- Continually evaluate how the training is going, and
- Alter training content and schedule as needed to meet the training objectives

Test workers to ensure readiness to change

OK, so you can't imagine a Director who yells, "Show Time!" before having a full dress rehearsal in which she grades each actor's readiness for opening night. Hopefully, you also can't imagine your airline pilot announcing to his expectant passengers: "I'm really excited about this trip in our new Boeing 787! This will be the first time I've flown this baby!"

For successful organizational change, we want to test each individual to ensure his capability to perform at the needed level. We have seen organizations where the very use of the word "test" sends off shock waves among the employees … and in some cases among employee advocates. We use the word "test" to mean the same thing that the Director does when he views a rehearsal and identifies those actors that need further role development and/or practice. The rehearsal provides information to the Director about what additional coaching and/or repetition she needs to bring to the theater company in transition.

We have also found that it is a good idea to record the training that people have completed and when they pass the proficiency test for the upcoming work.

ROBERT CUYLER, PHD AND DUTCH HOLLAND, PHD

We want to make a permanent record of training and tested performance level. We have had these training records come in handy when we were working with change leaders to understand exactly where they were in a change project they were running or inheriting.

Northwest Memorial Example:
Train All Employees in Their New Roles

The Telemedicine Coordinator scheduled video conferences with each of the telemedicine physicians and nurse 'tele-presenters' for both a technical and clinical orientation. Basic operation of equipment was covered, including initiating/ receiving calls and operation of pan/tilt/zoom features. Where necessary, lighting and camera angle were modified.

The 'tele-presenters' followed a script to practice introducing the telemedicine experience to patients. Members of the psychiatry project additionally tested home office telemedicine systems, running on hospital laptop computers, to establish that patient-care-grade connectivity was possible from home settings. The home office settings were carefully examined to make sure that privacy protection was in place for clinical examinations from these locations.

DID YOU NOTICE

1. Think about and prepare training for all employees. Northwest showed up with a script! Bravo!
2. Training workers at their stations beats the classroom any day. It might take a bit of logistics work, but it will be worth it.
3. Notice how Northwest used the training sessions to test equipment and validate office and privacy requirements.

Medi-Tel Example:
Train All Employees in Their New Roles

Some of the most critical training needed for Medi-Tel was coordination between the practice schedulers and customers. As the company was founded on principles of rapid, professional response, the interface between a customer requesting a consultation and Medi-Tel was critical. Scheduling for the new entity was unfamiliar to the schedulers and involved third parties (a customer representative) rather than a patient. Since 24 hour response and potentially worldwide customer base were a part of the endeavor, the scheduling team now had to share calls to provide around the clock response. The IT team decided that a customized, private email interface was the best solution, an application was written to enable a tablet interface for the schedule.

Faced with the challenge of training personnel who are employed by customers, Medi-Tel decided to create a series of training videos and competency checklists for customer personnel who would interface with the company. Modules were created for scheduling, medical record management, and tele-presenting. Additional resources were created for a number of specialty examinations, with a focus on use of telemedicine peripheral devices as well as assistance with medical examinations conducted by the physicians. Examples included nurse-assistance with neurological exams and protocols for measuring/imaging lesions for emergency and dermatology consultations. These resources were intended to supplement, not replace in-person training of tele-presenters.

DID YOU NOTICE

1. Finding critical processes and problematic interfaces and then building those training modules first is not a bad idea!
2. Make sure to train from the start of a task to the end of a task so the worker will get the workflow with the customer and the patient.
3. Notice the investment in time and money the company made to ensure their vendor was off to a good start. Bravo, Medi-Tel!

Requirement 4D: Identify and alter the system for monitoring performance

Mind-Clearing Examples – Imagine a Director who watches a dozen rehearsals of the new play without giving any feedback to the cast. Or imagine a Director who schedules a rehearsal but who doesn't leave his office to attend it.

ROBERT CUYLER, PHD AND DUTCH HOLLAND, PHD

> *Imagine the Director saying after the rehearsal, "I want you to get your feedback from your fellow performers."*
>
> *Or imagine a Director who says, "Let's just wait for the audience to give us feedback on how we are doing! They're the best judges anyway!"*

When workers start doing work that is relatively new to them, they need to know how well they are doing. If they do not know how they are doing, their performance may suffer because of uncertainty and/or doubt. Or they may conclude that since they are getting no feedback to the contrary, what they are doing must be right on target! This step in altering the performance management system is all about getting information to workers so that they can feel more comfortable about their work and continue to improve performance.

When workers are in existing jobs for any period of time, they know where they are performance wise because of the measures provided on the job or from routine feedback from customers or fellow employees. When workers are moved to new or different roles, these old ways of getting feedback are disrupted. Therefore, one of the tasks of the change leader is to ensure that there are means put in place for workers in new jobs to understand how well they are doing and what parts of the job they need to do better.

The most important mechanisms for getting feedback to employees who are new to work are as follows: supervisor input, measurable goals, just-in-time assessment and training, and customer/peer feedback.

- **Supervisor input:** The primary feedback mechanism for new or altered worker performance is the opinion and judgment of the worker's supervisor. Just as the stage performer looks to the Director for signals that she is performing the role as needed in the play, workers look to their bosses to ensure that they are on the right track. If an organization is systematically Engineering Organizational Change, they will have ensured that managers (the bosses) are on board with the change and able to give input to employees who are doing new work. While employee are personally responsible for developing their new roles, we openly encourage bosses involved in change to be aggressive about giving workers feedback ... after all, it's the boss' job to direct the play!

It is also the boss' job to answer questions … and the more comfortable the boss makes employees feel about the new work situation, the more questions he will get!

- **Measurable goals:** We talked in an earlier step about workers needing performance goals for the new or altered roles they were being asked to play. For goals to be useful in letting people know where they are, measurements must be taken and fed back in a timely manner (real-time is best). It does no good to provide quarterly, even monthly, feedback on progress toward goals. Workers in changed organizations need to know how they are doing on at least a weekly basis.

- **Just-in-time assessment and training:** Another form of feedback can come from the training resources who have helped workers prepare for the new or altered roles. We recommend that trainers who understand the altered work processes and FET make frequent passes through the work force to see how they are doing (a very informal role) or to conduct spot assessments or audits of training results (a much more formal role). We have seen organizations put their trainers on call to answer questions from workers in new roles.

- **Customer/peer feedback:** Frequently workers will get feedback from their peers, either verbally or by watching other members of the organization do similar work. We recommend that supervisors encourage workers to talk to their peers to better understand how things are going, for themselves and others. We have seen companies sponsor lunch meetings of small groups of employees to enable conversation among workers who were coming up to speed on new jobs. Sometimes workers get feedback from their customers on how things are going, although we do not encourage it. We want the workers to know what they are doing without having to ask their customers for a grade!

Before we leave this step, it is important to note that formal performance appraisal and salary review systems are rarely of value for job feedback during an organizational change. These formal systems are frequently tied to an annual calendar, and are to be used to give long-term feedback on how the employee is doing overall in what might be a string of altered roles. After an organizational change has been in place for some time, then the formal systems are of great value for giving feedback about how the worker performed in the past review period.

Northwest Memorial Example: Identify and alter the system for monitoring performance

For the rural hospitals, the issue was not to alter the performance management system but to re-activate it. The performance management system administered by Human Resources was good enough but had not been put to disciplined use by the managers involved in many aspects of surgery.

Changes were made to performance evaluation forms for the surgical nurses who would coordinate the pre- and post-op consultations to include performance criteria related to patient satisfaction for the services that would be provided at the rural hospitals. Criteria for merit increases were expanded to address satisfaction scores that exceeded expectations for patient satisfaction variables related to timeliness of appointment and 'staff helped me feel at ease and my questions were answered adequately'.

DID YOU NOTICE

1. A change effort without a performance management and feedback process is like a ship without a rudder.
2. Changing job descriptions, as the companies did earlier, requires a change in the performance management and appraisal systems.

Medi-Tel Example: Identify and alter the system for monitoring performance

Formal job descriptions were drafted for the telemedicine physicians, including a separate model for contract/part-time physicians. The full-time physicians reviewed the drafts and made recommendations for how the balance for patient care and administrative/business development roles were defined.

Additions were made to the performance evaluation forms of the group practice staff who would support Medi-Tel. Each employee was also given a time sheet to record work activity related to Medi-Tel activities, so that a determination could be made when Medi-Tel needed to create dedicated jobs to cover these support functions as Medi-Tel's business expanded.

DID YOU NOTICE

1. Performance evaluations and timesheets were put in place for continuous usage in the firm.
2. Notice how non-personal data from evaluation forms and timesheets can be used for the planning of future jobs.

Requirement 4E: Alter and communicate compensation payoffs

> *Mind-Clearing Example – Imagine an actor who goes on stage for opening night of the new play wearing his old costume and singing his favorite song from the last play. Imagine the Director saying, "Well, your performance is not really what I expected or wanted ... but here is your paycheck anyway."*
>
> *Mind-Clearing Example – Or imagine an actor who gets his first paycheck after starting rehearsals for a new play. Imagine the actor complaining to the producer and director that the amount of the check did not match his newly-negotiated compensation contract ... and then hearing, "We decided not to change paychecks right now for anybody in the theater company; changing the numbers would just be confusing and too much work for our accounting staff."*

When workers start doing work that is relatively new to them, they need to see and understand how that new work is related to how they get paid. Working people follow the money. We all work for pay. Money counts. Show them where the money is ... and where the money is not ... and they will direct themselves toward the money and away from the deficit.

The challenge for the change leader is to compensate employees for the work that matches the new way of doing business ... and to not compensate for work that no longer aligns with the new way of doing business! The compensation

ROBERT CUYLER, PHD AND DUTCH HOLLAND, PHD

principles that apply in transitioning workers from an old way of working to a new one are as follows:

- Compensation is earned when performance, as defined in the newly-altered role, is delivered at the level agreed-to in the agreement with the boss (the organization).

- Continued performance of the old role after change-over to the new way of doing business should result in counseling and reprimand that will have a negative impact on the worker's performance review.

We have found no more difficult job than convincing change leaders and managers alike that the organization must pay for the work needed from employees ... and rigorously address non-performance of new roles and expectations. While this sounds simple enough, it is very difficult to get managers in some companies to act in this emotion-laden area of performance management.

The need to match pay and performance is easier to see in the case of vendors or contract employees. No capable manager would pay contract employees for doing work that was no longer a part of the current statement of work in the vendor's contract. (Imagine defending yourself to your boss if you did!) And no capable manager would go forward with new vendor contracts and then refuse to pay except under the terms of the old contract.[4]

Unfortunately, it is very common to see change leaders and managers acting as though it is "business as usual" even though the workers have declined to embrace their new roles in the changed organization. Paying workers even though they do not change their roles sends an immediate signal to these workers and those around them that doing business the new way is not required or desired. So, there are actions that need to be taken to ensure the compensation system "pays off for change" and "doesn't pay off for failure to change." These steps involve mechanically changing the payoff rules in the company's performance management system ... and then following the company rules for performance appraisal and compensation with a great deal of discipline.

---

4   Compensation rules and laws are sometimes tricky. Do not do anything that communicates compensation changes without the blessing of the appropriate Human Resource specialist for your company. Tell HR the principle you want to change or put in place, and let HR tell you how your desired changes can be done legally and fairly.

Align the payoff rules with the new and altered roles

The idea of payoff rules is simple. We want to have a set of rules or guidelines that tell us what to pay and when to pay it for different performance levels. For a vendor, we have terms in his contract that state that he will be paid after certain specified work has been satisfactorily completed. The specified work is normally listed right in the contract so there is no confusion about what work goes with what pay. In some vendor contracts, we find incentive compensation – extra dollars that the vendor might receive if the work is done in some exceptional way. Normally, the criteria for deciding on the extra incentive compensation are listed in detail.

For employees, such payoff rules are more often implied than written into an explicit contract between worker and employing organization. The payoff rule normally followed by a company is that the worker is due his agreed-to monthly compensation when he satisfactorily performs the work called for in his job (as documented sometimes in a job description). In some companies that offer incentive compensation, additional dollars might be won by the employee by achieving certain goals or targets. Many companies write down these targets at the beginning of the target period (usually a year) so that they can make any incentive compensation calculations needed at the end of the year after work results are available for evaluation.

The change leader's job is to cause the old job description that drove salary to be replaced with the new job description of the altered role that now drives salary. In addition, the change leader must ensure that all "old goals" in the files or paperwork have been replaced by the new goals that go with the altered roles.

This is not rocket science … but the details count! If we have thirty workers moving to altered roles and goals, somebody needs to ensure that there are thirty altered job descriptions and sets of goals inserted in the company's files in place of thirty old role descriptions and goal sets. This paperwork change is absolutely necessary so that the company's accountants who ensure that everyone in the company gets the right check written for the right person at the right time can do that accurately.

ROBERT CUYLER, PHD AND DUTCH HOLLAND, PHD

Follow the payoff rules on a day-to-day basis

Changing the paperwork is a key first step to ensuring that the organization will pay for the performance it wants and not pay for performance it does not want. But the critical ingredient that makes the pay for performance linkage work is the boss. Which boss? Every boss! Every boss in the organization must follow the payoff rules to the letter to ensure that employees all align their behavior with the vision. Every boss must:

- **Coach workers toward performance on the mark:** The boss' job is to ensure that the workers on his watch are moving toward peak performance in altered roles ... using altered work processes with altered FET ... to achieve the new way of doing business. The boss' goal should be to win for the company while coaching each employee in how to win for himself.

- **Give real-time feedback for performance off the mark:** When a boss sees performance off the mark (not aligned with the vision), she should give real-time feedback to the worker to give him the chance to get back on track. More coaching might be required to show the worker how to do that or to provide the training needed to get the worker's skills to the desired level.

- **Provide coaching and counseling for performance off the mark:** For workers whose performance is repeatedly off the mark, the boss should provide what we call "counseling"... exploring with the employee the reasons why performance does not comply with the direction in the vision ... or the coaching. The goal would be to assist the worker in the steps needed to get back or track ... or to consider leaving the organization or role.

- **Put jobs at risk for those employees consistently off the mark:** If a worker is not willing to perform to the mark, the boss has no choice but to tell the employee that his employment is at risk. That is, the boss says, "You have not demonstrated the kind or level of performance this organization is willing to pay for ... therefore we are putting you on probation..." Most companies already have a policy or procedure for dealing with unsatisfactory performance. In situations like this, the boss should work directly with her Human Resources Department to ensure that her intentions and needs are met within the organization's guidelines.

- **Remove employees who do not comply:** Organizations that want to master change to deal with today's turbulent business environment must be willing to take firm action. Failure to remove someone from the organization who refuses to go along with an organizational change can send a message to other workers that will cripple the organization's future change capability. Our experience is that one clearly-justified removal in an organization is a powerful message that the officially-announced organizational change is truly not optional!

Northwest Memorial Example: Alter and Communicate Compensation Payoffs

This step was particularly difficult for Memorial Northwest because salaried physicians were involved. Half of the psychiatrists were definitely not happy about the change to a expanded evening and weekend call obligations. They were just "agin it" from the beginning.

The urban hospital had a precedent for paid call in orthopedics and neurosurgery, and the CMO proposed a modest 'on call' stipend for evening and weekend call, supplemented by a per-case fee for tele-psychiatry consults that followed the approved referral protocols. The participating hospitals agreed to cover these fees in order to improve ED length of stay and sitter costs. In addition to the 'carrot approach', the psychiatry section chief made it clear in section meetings that he expected his doctors to 'get with the program' now that paid call was in place; feedback from the hospitals and the Mobile Crisis Team and timeliness of physician response would be part of annual performance evaluations.

Medi-Tel Example: Alter and Communicate Compensation Payoffs

With assistance from the Advisory Board and attorney, Mr. Ames drew up a compensation plan for the owner physicians. A base salary was determined for each predicated on a volume of in-person and telemedicine visits monthly. A bonus structure was formulated

ROBERT CUYLER, PHD AND DUTCH HOLLAND, PHD

based on a combination of business development success, customer satisfaction, and overall margin for the business. Support staff (scheduling and IT) who would take on-call duties had a daily on-call payment added to salary.

DID YOU NOTICE

1. Northwest paid for what they wanted. Another way to say it is that Northwest aligned performance and compensation.
2. Workers will be "unhappy with compensation" until the rules are worked out, communicated and judged to be fair … for the business and the workers.

And in conclusion …

The mechanism used to transition actors from one play to the next is the "contract" that formalizes the agreement between actor and theater company to work together, under certain terms, in the next play.

For successful organizational change, employees must be under agreement to perform to the new vision of the organization. In addition, all employees must be under contract for the process of transitioning to the new vision, during which they will be

- performing their normal, routine duties for the current way of operating while
- performing the work necessary to transition to the company's new way of operating.

Failing to alter the performance management system while expecting successful organizational change is akin to expecting the performance of a new play from actors who are still under exclusive contract for performing the old play!

For successful organization change, there must be physical alteration of the business system that the organization uses to direct and reinforce the performance of its managers and employees. This performance management system is the organization's mechanism for procuring, directing, and retaining the kind of performance it needs. This performance management system must be altered in order to (1) reinforce the transition to the new organizational future and (2) to dis-incentivize failure to transition to the new future.

CHAPTER SIX

Manage Change as a Project

> *Mind-Clearing Example – Imagine the Director who has identified the new play and the opening date but who has developed no action plans for the weeks of work needed to transition from the old play to the new.*
>
> *Imagine the theater company not knowing when final role assignments were to be made, when new costumes were to be fitted, when rehearsals were to be held, when the sets needed to be completed, when the stage rigging would be tested, and so on.*
>
> *When asked about the schedule for key transition events, the Director answers, "I'm busy worrying about the long-term future of our theater company ... and I certainly don't have time to work through the kinds of details you all seem to be so worried about!"*

THE VISION OF the desired way of working clearly provides guidance for direction of the organizational change. But time spent gazing into a future (that will always have some mystery in it) can be wasted if immediate and obvious actions at hand cannot be taken. Requirement five of organizational change is to construct and fully communicate project action plans and schedules for change work for each week or month of the organizational change. (Change work is defined as tasks that must be accomplished for a change to occur, like training, installing and testing new equipment, writing procedure manuals, etc.). Organization members need specific plans and schedules that detail the week-by-week change work that must be completed to get to the new way of doing business. Workers must know what change work to do "on Monday morning" (and every other Monday morning) ... along with their "day jobs," the current work they are already doing.

For minor organizational change, the amount of change work to be done may be quite small, involving only a few workers or work processes. But for major organizational changes that will involve many workers (maybe thousands) and several work processes (maybe dozens), the amount of change work that must be completed can be huge and overwhelming! Without at least weekly scheduling of specific change work to do, the organizational change effort will just bog down as organization members focus their time and energy on their current day jobs of producing products and seeing patients.

Manage organizational change like a project

We have used the word "project" several times in this book ... but not with the degree of emphasis needed for effective organizational change. We mean to treat change work as a real project that has an identity as well as a manager with the authority and resources needed to get it finished. We mean that change work must be managed with the discipline of project management ... a specialized and well-developed management field that deals with getting unique work done in an organized, systematic manner ... on target, on time and on budget. In this chapter on using project management for change, we unabashedly state that change work must be subjected to disciplined management ... and the closest developed capability to what is needed here is project management.

The master schedule has its place in the overall timetable and sequence of activities associated with organizational change. While that place may vary, companies that have mastered change put the project charter and the master schedule as the first steps and use them to guide change leadership all the way from vision development to the final celebration of success.

The general sequence of work to be managed in an organizational change project is as follows:

1. **Chartering the organizational change as a project:** The executive who is commissioning the organizational change should appoint a formal project manager and give him his first assignment of developing the formal charter for the change project. The project charter is the executive's and project manager's concise statement of the intent, goals, scope, change budget, limits of and responsibilities for the organizational change.

2. **Development, approval and communication of the master schedule:** The project manager sketches the beginning and desired end points of

ROBERT CUYLER, PHD AND DUTCH HOLLAND, PHD

the organizational change, develops the task list, creates the first high-level master schedule, and seeks schedule approval by the executive in charge of the change.

> ### The Shock and Awe of Organizational Change
>
> *The first cut at a master schedule can produce big surprises for organizational leadership -- when the first schedule reveals the realities of the upcoming change. The draft schedule shows the time and people involved, the number of steps that must be taken and managed, the resources that will be required, etc. In short, now senior management can see for the first time all the change work that must be completed while the organization continues to do its "day job" of serving customers and seeing patients.*

3. **Development of the vision and the case for organizational change:** The change leader launches those activities needed to develop in some detail the vision (i.e., the new way the organization will be doing business in the future) as well as the case for change.

4. **Initial communication of the vision and case for change:** The change leader begins the communication process designed to give the organization a heads up to changes that are to be made along with the reasons for those changes.

5. **Identification of change work, that is, the alterations that will need to be made:** The change leader names teams to identify needed alterations in

   - **Work processes**
   - **Facilities, equipment, technology (FET)**
   - **Performance management system** (e.g., worker roles, training, etc.)

6. **Development and communication of a detailed master schedule:** A detailed master schedule is created to show the calendar for completing all needed Change Work.

7. **Alteration of worker roles:** the change leader authorizes bosses to conduct one-on-one contracting with workers for

- **Starting the new way of working** at the targeted, change-over time
- **Continuing to perform work** as it is currently done until change-over
- **Completing the change work** required for change over (e.g., participating in training, new role development, new equipment break-in, etc.)

8. **Conducting change work:** Many consider this step as the heart of organization change, where existing work processes are studied, re-designed, and then altered to fit the change vision; where FET is analyzed and actions taken to modify it or to buy and install new FET; and where roles are altered and training delivered, and so on. This step alone can take weeks to months of hard work for some organization members while other members are uninvolved, continuing to conduct today's business as usual ... until that first training class appears on their schedules.

9. **Verifying all change work:** The change leader ensures all the needed change work has been done, including alteration of work processes, FET, and roles ... and that tests have been conducted to ensure that all needed alterations have been adequately made.

10. **Changing over to the new way of doing business:** At a specific time(s) the various parts of the organization make the switch from doing work the old way to doing work the new way.

11. **Break-in (or learning-curve phase) and stabilization:** The change leader aggressively leads during the first few weeks/months of working the new way, during which the organization continues to learn and make further refinements to work processes, FET, and worker roles to achieve the desired way of doing business.

Leadership for the change project

If change work must be managed like a project and special attention must be given to the management of all the risks, who is the project manager? The project manager is the official, formal, organization-chart leader of the organization that is making the change. Only the big boss, the CEO, has the final authority to put an organizational change into effect.

ROBERT CUYLER, PHD AND DUTCH HOLLAND, PHD

While the boss cannot escape the ultimate accountability for organizational change and for the management of the change project, she can use able assistants to help. These assistants can be most helpful if they have project management skills and experience. In fact, starting a big organizational change effort without an experienced project management professional in a key support role is an almost certain recipe for change that will be ... off target, off schedule, and way over budget.

It is still interesting to us as consultants to see managers who would not dare tackle the construction of a major capital asset without a professional-level, project management firm ... move forward with a multi-million dollar organizational change without an experienced project management professional somewhere in the loop!

A project management professional who will be put in charge of an organizational change must know all the "mechanical stuff" about project management: building and documenting the project plan, ensuring that all required resources are assigned to the project and clearly tasked, monitoring and reporting on project performance (i.e., schedule, cost, quality and risk), managing project interdependencies, and so on.

But in addition, the following skills, experiences, and sensitivities are critical for the success of the organizational change and the project manager:

- **Cognizance of "run the business, change the business"**

Organizational change does not occur in a vacuum but while the current business is running at full speed. The Project manager must be able to take into account the run-the-business situation and flex change project planning to ensure that there will be enough executive focus and energy to keep the project moving. For example, the project manager who insists that the executive team meet this week for the regular monthly change status report while the executives are fighting a major quality issue that has just arisen is going to lose credibility and stature by being just plain dumb.

- **Knowledge of the company and the industry in which it competes**

In many mature industries, the differences between success and failure are very small and hard to see or appreciate by anyone who does not have "the business in his bones." A mechanical project manager with no touch or feel for the business or for her organization cannot do the change job well enough for success. While the project manager cannot know everything about the business, she needs to be able to discern the subject matter expertise that needs to be added to the project. She does not need to know everything, but she needs to know where to find everything that needs knowing.

- **Willingness to call a spade a spade in front of the CEO and her executive team**

Regardless of the potential bounty of an organizational change, sailing will not always be smooth. Managers are, after all, paid to be biased in the direction of the functions they represent, and they are not always eager to make needed changes in their units when maybe it's the other guy's unit that should be making changes. So there will be issues and conflicts that can only be resolved around the executive table with the CEO in charge. The project manager, as the guy who has to put issues on that table, cannot be hesitant or shy about pointing out risks or about escalating issues to the top.

- **Excellent interpersonal and communication skills**

We have all heard the saying that "if you cannot measure it, you cannot manage it." For organizational change we can add the saying "if you cannot say it, you cannot lead it." The Project manager must be able to communicate clearly and intelligently, and be able to describe the desired organizational change and what must be done to successfully complete the change. Having good interpersonal skills will also be essential to lead organization members to do the right things at the right time.

After reading this section of the chapter, some have said that we are asking for superman (or woman) to be the project manager of an organizational change. Are we? Changing the direction of a multi-billion dollar organization with a few thousand employees scattered over a hundred or so countries is not a task for just anyone. Supermen (and women) are rare and to be valued when available. When superheroes are scarce, however, we believe that competent, well-focused project managers can use the methodology outlined in this book to produce super results.

This chapter is all about getting in control of the needed change work so that the desired organizational change can be made … on target, on time, and on budget. Getting change work under control requires a project management mindset, a robust planning and scheduling method, critical path planning, valid work breakdown structures and task lists, weekly schedules, and several one-on-one meetings with the workers involved in the change. And as a critical overlay, getting change work under control means explicit and disciplined risk management.

Figure 6.1: Risks to manage in an organization change

Managing risks in an organizational change project

Taking an organization that is doing work one way and changing that organization to work in another way is not an easy or certain exercise. Therefore, a critical project management discipline is risk management. The size of the risks in an organizational change can be anything from a few thousand dollars for small changes to hundreds of millions for potential disruption to a large organization or to its customers.

There are many risks along the way ... risks that must be explicitly and aggressively managed for the change to be successfully completed. We have identified three categories of risks that must be managed during the process of organizational change:

- **Technical risk:** the chance that various parts of the organization will not work the way they were planned to work. Technical failure could be needed equipment that does not work as intended (or advertised), work processes that do not achieve the desired result, and so on. Imagine the props in a new theater production functioning so poorly that attention is diverted away from the actors!

- **Organizational risk:** the chance organization members will not accept the change to the new way of doing business. Imagine actors on the stage for a new performance who clearly do not have their hearts in the play and who give only half-hearted performances!

- **Business risk:** the chance the costly-to-implement organizational change will not pay off in dollars and cents. Failure to gain a favorable business outcome could be caused by a number of factors, from poor design of the change (presenting a new way of working that customers do not like) to flawed implementation (causing even a good organizational change design to feel wrong to customers and employees alike). Imagine a new performance of a musical comedy that is well executed by the cast ... but that just isn't funny enough to continue selling seats!

We doubt that there is an experienced worker anywhere who has not seen an organizational change that either did not work, from a technical point of view, was not used, or, if used, made no money for the organization. Unfortunately, that kind of comprehensive risk management is a tall order for many of today's organizations that generally focus on technical issue resolution alone while organizational and business risks are left to chance. The organizational change message is very clear – plan to manage all three kinds of risks effectively – or keep your present way of doing business in play. Moving ahead toward a new way of doing business without managing all three risks is a certain recipe for organizational disruption and even disaster.

Identify and dispel deadly assumptions that will disable project management

The idea of using project management as a disciplined way of guiding a transition to a new way of doing business is hard to dismiss. But for line managers who spend their time running the daily business, the whole idea of project management is just what it is … an idea. Project management as a discipline is a very different way of managing than most managers have experienced.

Project management is needed because a transition to a new way of doing business is a "unique deliverable," exactly what project management delivers. In a transition, the organization needs to be operating in the new way on target, on time and on budget, requiring planning and control skills not normally found in line managers. We have seen the most success when experienced project managers were brought into change projects to guide and keep track of the many steps that will need to be taken before the organizational change is complete.

Step	Change-Blocking Assumption	Disabling Behavior by Management	Proven Consequences
Requirement Five: Project Management of Transition Projects	People manage themselves every day, and they will manage themselves through this change	Missing or inadequate day-to-day plans and schedules for organized preparation and implementation of change	• Uneven implementation • False starts • Inconsistent results

Change leaders can spot the likely presence of deadly assumptions through conversations heard about what needs to be done to get the change completed or to get project management into place. Hearing the suggestion to "just let people move at their own pace; you know, some of us are busier than others" calls for the change leader to surface deadly assumptions and to dispel them in any way possible, starting with the proven consequences in the table above.

Take these action steps to use project management for transition

Now we are on to the hard work of managing the overall organizational change with the following five steps: Skip a step and expect expensive delays.

> ### Use project management for transition
>
> - 5A: Develop project charter for executive approval
> - 5B: Set and communicate master schedule
> - 5C: Use week-at-a-time implementation scheduling with one-on-one assignments
> - 5D: Regularly measure transition progress and re-schedule as needed
> - 5E: Confirm, stabilize and celebrate the completed transition to the new way of doing business

Requirement 5A: Develop project charter for executive approval

> *Mind-Clearing Example – Imagine a Director who makes an oral presentation to the Producer and investors about his desire to put on a new play to replace the current one. When asked about the details of the new play or about a document that describes his proposed project, the Director says, "I haven't had time to work out any details ... and I sure don't want to waste any time writing stuff down. I just want to get your approval for the play so I can get started. As we work through the details, perhaps I can have my assistant brief you if you like."*

The trick is to look at all the needed change work as a project. The project must be managed to get the needed change work done in an organized and systematic way – while the organization carries on with its current way of doing business: making products, serving clients, seeing patients, etc. The first step, and some would say, the single most important step for getting the needed change work done is to develop a project charter containing basic information that can be used to steer the entire change project.

A Project Charter is a formal document that describes the purpose or intent of the organizational change, the way the change project will be structured and how it will be successfully implemented. A fully-functional project charter will describe:

ROBERT CUYLER, PHD AND DUTCH HOLLAND, PHD

- What we are trying to do with the change: vision, scope, objectives and deliverables
- How we will accomplish the change: approach, methods, milestones, budgets, resources
- Who will be involved in the change: stakeholders, executive in charge, project manager and her roles and responsibilities

The project charter should be first drafted by the project manager after extensive conversations with the executives who believe the change is necessary. The project manager may not get the information he needs from simple conversations so he should be prepared to ask prepared questions to obtain needed information. Frequently organizational changes are ignited by a study, a task force report, or an executive retreat. In that case, the project manager should ask for any materials that came from such formal efforts: studies, minutes of meetings, wall charts or whatever was used to record the thinking behind the organizational change.

The components of the project charter

Before we dive into the nuts and bolts of the charter, let's review a bit. An organization's executive leadership has deliberated and concluded that their organization needs to change some aspects of the way it is doing business. While there is executive direction (perhaps, a high-level vision) and intent, there is not as yet any organized way of making that change happen, hopefully, on target, on time, and on budget. If the CEO shouted to the entire organization, "Here is our high level vision for the future ... let's get started tomorrow," most would likely predict a certain amount of paralysis mixed with pandemonium as the order of the day.

This chapter, this part of the successful organizational change process, is designed to explain how to take a high-level vision and develop action plans that will enable the change to be made in an organized and predictable way ... on target, on time, and on budget. That is a tall order in anybody's book. The project charter serves as the foundation for the organizational change and should contain the following information.

1. **The purpose and/or intent** of the change
2. **The specific objectives** and deliverables of the change
3. **The scope of the change**, what parts of the organization will be affected
4. **The change approach** including high level phases and milestones

5. **The implementation steps** for the change
6. **The stakeholders** in the change
7. **The leadership roles** and responsibilities in the change
8. **The budget** for the change

The list above is not a strict formula, and change leaders can get by with a few more or a few less components, as long as the entries to those sections are valid. Better yet, templates for project charters are available for download from the web. While the templates are different, some provide almost fool-proof instructions for completing them. But caution is needed.

> *Beware of the holes in any template*
>
> *Most of the sections of a project charter can be filled in with the information at hand. There are no right or wrong answers to sections like "goals, scope or stakeholders." But there are right or wrong (valid or invalid) answers to the following sections:*
>
> - *the approach,*
> - *implementation steps, and*
> - *leadership roles and responsibilities.*
>
> *The purpose of this book is to give valid information for those three sections. Failure to use valid information will produce a charter that is likely to lead to an unsuccessful organizational change. Fore-warned is fore-armed!*

The change approach and implementation steps

This part of the charter is critical because it is where the rubber meets the road for organizational change. In this section of the charter, the change leader or the project manager describes the approach (i.e., change project phases) and the implementation steps to be used to complete the project. Once the charter is approved by top management, the project manager is bound to the approved steps that become the recipe for the change. A summary of the action steps we have covered is shown in condensed form in Appendix A: Task List for Successful Organizational Change.

ROBERT CUYLER, PHD AND DUTCH HOLLAND, PHD

The organization of the project

The leadership roles and responsibilities for the project are also critical in the
charter. The way the change leadership is organized can make the difference
between success and failure of the organizational change. Three leadership
configurations are shown below; one will make change possible while the other
two will likely stop or dilute any change efforts.

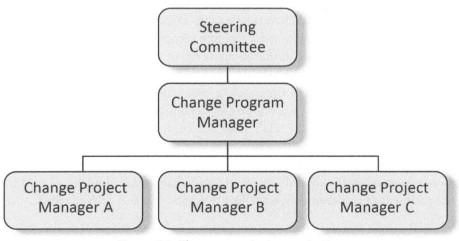

Figure 5.1: The pure project organization

The logical place to start, and where many others stop, is the pure project organization as shown in figure 5.1. This figure shows how multiple projects might fit under a master project or program. This figure is clearly a valuable part of the organization needed for project success. But any change project is going to be carried out while the organization carries on with its regular business of producing today's products and serving today's customers. How will this work? Is the organizational change to be firmly anchored in thin air?

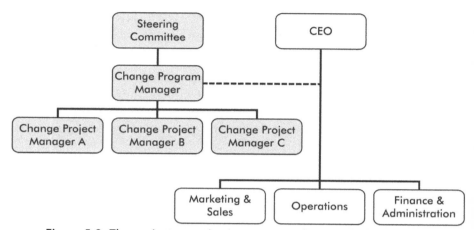

Figure 5.2: The project organization connected to steering committee

Figure 5.2 shows the project organization connected to the day-to-day organizational structure for running the business. There are two important aspects of this figure to note. First note that the program manager, to whom all projects report, has a dotted line relationship directly to the CEO with a solid line relationship to what is called a steering committee. Such an arrangement frequently has a steering committee made up of senior functional managers who report to the CEO on a day-to-day business. While serving on the steering committee, each manager is expected to "wear his organization or enterprise hat" rather than being a representative of his unit only. Looks good but there is still a problem because there is a solid line connection between the steering committee and the Change Program Manager, meaning that those functional managers have ultimate control over change projects that will surely involve their own organizations. Such an arrangement will likely result in informal political bargaining that can keep a change effort from have the full desired effect.

ROBERT CUYLER, PHD AND DUTCH HOLLAND, PHD

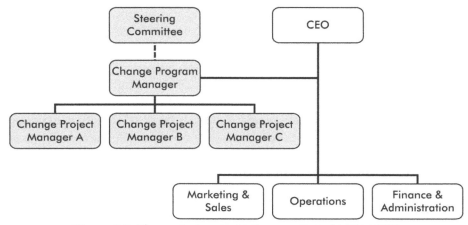

Figure 5.3: The project organization connected to the CEO

Figure 5.3 also shows the project organization connected to the day-to-day organizational structure for running the business but in this organizational design, the steering committee can provide input to the program manager but they cannot make a final decision about a change issue. That responsibility rests with the CEO only as shown by the solid line between himself and the program manager. In practice, once everybody understands the lay of the land from a structure point of view, the steering committee usually plays nice and as a result, the program manager does not have to take too many issues to the CEO. However, with this arrangement, the threat of the CEO becoming involved in an issue is a constant reminder for the steering committee to always wear their organizational hats rather than individually wearing their functional hats.

The key to executive approval

The key to gaining executive approval of the project charter is to not show him the charter. How is that for logic? The rationale goes like this, executives want to approve a charter that looks and feels like the latest discussion they had with other executives about the organizational change. The details of a well-developed charter look to them like "just more bureaucracy" and will cool off the desire to get the right organizational change going.

We use the contents of the project charter as well as the contents of any planning notes or documents to construct a presentation for executive approval. Our presentation is designed to say or convey several key messages:

- **We heard your intent**: Your intent is what is guiding our change project The idea here is to be sure that the executive hears his words coming back to him. The executive should be able to say, "Yep, that is what I was talking about!" As soon as the executive recognizes the project manager's alignment, the project manager's credibility goes up.

- **We have done our homework:** The executive should hear that the project manager has done extensive analysis and planning for the organizational change. A slide that shows who has been consulted in the organization about what subject will do wonders to build credibility if, and only if, the names on the list are the "A" players in the organization.

- **We are ready to rock and roll:** The executive should hear that the project manager has covered all the bases to ensure that stakeholders know what is going on, what their stake is, and what they will be responsible for completing.

- **We do have some issues:** The issues confronting the project managers can be listed at this time along with a suggested solution for each issue. It is critical not to show an issue that does not have one or more solutions ready to be approved. If a presented issue does not have an immediate solution in the room, the project manager should not leave the room until there is agreement on who and how the issue will be resolved as well as whether or not the project must wait for issue resolution or can start in anticipation of a successful resolution of the issue.

- **Just say the word, Boss:** The executive should feel that the project manager is "straining at the leash." The executive should see, hear and feel the project manager's alignment with the intent of the change, her passion, her readiness, and her confidence that the change is under good control.

We could tell horror stories here about project managers who translate the executive's words into "change-speak," using change management and behavioral science terms that mean nothing to the executive but do cause him to question the competence of the project manager. The presentation to executives that seeks approval of the project charter is a "big casino" pitch; failure in this presentation may have many negative consequences including slowing the organizational change, confusing those in the presentation, and/or costing the project managers her job.

ROBERT CUYLER, PHD AND DUTCH HOLLAND, PHD

Northwest Memorial Example:
Develop project charter for executive approval

The project charter for the Telemedicine Initiative was worked out with the team that had been formed by the Chief Medical Officer. The intent and rationale along with the vision and scope of the change were worked out "under combat conditions" as each member of the team presented his or her ideas about the charter. Phrases like, "Well, what my people will need out of this are so and so" were voiced by each team member as they tried to best represent their constituents.

After several rounds of comments, the team realized that they needed to put on their "institutional hats" rather than their department hats, and soon moved to agreements on the most critical parts of the project charter. The Chief Medical Officer secured the final approval of the project charter in a one-on-one meeting with the CEO. After hearing the intent of the change and the rationale, the CEO gave the approval signal, "Let's go for it!" The three target specialties were expected to be the pilot projects for a greater future role for telemedicine, and the CEO wanted to establish clinical quality, organizational coordination/adjustment, and reputation for innovative care in the pilot applications that would establish a sound foundation for expansion.

DID YOU NOTICE

1. The Project Manager can lead the steering committee through the development of the project charter.
2. Leading the committee will be much easier if the project manager drafts the charter and sits with the committee while they discuss and red-line the draft.
3. Did you notice how the CEO inserted extra targets into the pilot to get data for another agenda, in this case, a business development agenda?

Medi-Tel Example:
Develop project charter for executive approval

Three months after Medi-Tel launched services with two initial clients, the owner doctors set up a weekend retreat with the company's Advisory Board. A central task of the weekend was to develop a finalized company charter. One important metric that was discussed was the proportion of traditional face-to-face medicine relative to telemedicine consultations. While the initial plan was formulated around the need to keep income flow for the doctors during the start-up period, it was clear that sticking to the old paradigm was interfering with new business development and critically-important contacts with customers. Without a more aggressive acquisition of new customers, Medi-Tel could die on the vine.

After much discussion, the group agreed to keep face-to-face medicine at a ceiling of quarter time for each doctor. To avert a "cash call" to keep the operations going, the partner doctors needed to step up their business development activities to accelerate finalized new accounts.

The intent and rationale along with the vision and scope of the change were worked out "under combat conditions" as each member of the team presented his or her ideas about the company's charter as a "pure play" telemedicine company. Advisory team members were much more consistent in their view that the company needed a laser focus on its core business if it was to grow and succeed. The input of the Advisors was sobering to the partners, and they agreed to trust the business experience and instincts of the Board. Dr. Janssen and Mr. Ames finalized the project charter in a one-to-one meeting and presented the final version in a closing meeting with all parties.

DID YOU NOTICE

1. A project charter is best written after the stakeholders have agreed on what they want from their enterprise.
2. Stakeholders who cannot come to agreement should not launch an enterprise.
3. Writing a draft project charter before stakeholder agreement can sometimes serve as a tool for gaining agreement.

ROBERT CUYLER, PHD AND DUTCH HOLLAND, PHD

Requirement 5B: Set and Communicate the Master Schedule for Change Work

> *Mind-Clearing Example – Imagine a Director who has no master schedule for the work to be done to transition her theater company from the old play to the new one.*
>
> *When asked about the calendar dates for key transition events (like contracting with actors, fitting costumes, conducting rehearsals, etc.), she answers, "Well the situation is much too fluid to put things down on a calendar. We'll just have to wait to see how things work out, won't we?"*

In the first four requirements for organizational change, we have identified much of the change work that will need to be done:

- We have a vision of a telemedicine practice that needs to be detailed and communicated to the organization,
- We have work process alterations that need to be made to implement the telemedicine practice,
- We have alterations/acquisitions to make in the organization's FET to support a telemedicine practice
- We have individual worker role alterations to make and contracting sessions to conduct so we have a telemedicine workforce ready to go

The trick is to look at all the needed change work as a project. The project must be managed to get the needed change work done in an organized and systematic way – while the organization carries on with its current way of doing business, making products, serving patients, etc. The single most important tool for getting the needed change work done is the master schedule ... which is driven by the work breakdown structure followed by the task list.

List of tasks to be completed

This book has been about detailing the steps in the work breakdown structure and task list for an organization change. The previous chapters provided the "nuts and bolts" actions associated with the four major work elements. Now it is up to the project manager to put those nut and bolt actions into a logical, master schedule that takes into account the realities of the organization that is to be changed. The actual schedule that will be constructed will not be exactly linear because of the need to accommodate organization dates, other major initiatives, and the priorities associated with the current business.

Figure 5.4: Work breakdown structure for project management of an organizational change

Critical attributes of the master schedule

Regardless of the magnitude of the organizational change, the master schedule should have the following attributes to be a sound base for managing an organizational change:

- **Comprehensiveness:** the master schedule must include all moving parts of the organizational change ... not just the most visible parts (like the purchase and installation of new telemedicine technology). Work process and worker role alterations, contracting sessions and training classes ... all must go on the master schedule!

- **Realism:** We have seen timetables for organizational change that are about as unrealistic as driving your SUV to the moon. Change work takes time and energy ... and must fit into or around the already busy schedules of the workers. Realistic time estimates for completing the different kinds of change work must be developed ... and then folded together if the change is to have any chance of being completed on target, on time, and on budget.

- **Business fit:** As we have said before, organizations do change work while they continue to do the organization's current work serving patients. Scheduling change work must take the schedule of old work into account if the change schedule is to be realistic. For example, scheduling work process alterations for an accounting organization while they are in the thick of preparing tax returns for an April 15 deadline is courting a schedule disaster! On the other hand, the master schedule must also take

ROBERT CUYLER, PHD AND DUTCH HOLLAND, PHD

into account the realities of the needed change. If the organization must have a change done by a certain date to maintain its level of profitability, that reality must be dealt with in the schedule.

- **Critical path schedule:** This kind of schedule shows what change work must be done in what order so that all the change work has the most time-efficient flow to it. For example, imagine trying to train employees on new equipment that has not yet arrived! The critical path method is a key discipline within project management and is an absolute requirement for projects that have more than a handful of change work steps.

When we finish explaining master scheduling to our change management clients, we frequently hear an attitude of, "Oh no! Do we really have to do all this detailed planning and scheduling work?" The simple answer is, "Only if you want to have a chance at bringing in your telemedicine implementation on target, on time, and on budget!" As we have said before, change management is not rocket science but it is engineering – disciplined, detailed, hard work! And using a detailed master schedule is a requirement for successful organizational change and for implementing a telemedicine practice.

Integrating project management and change management to set the master schedule

Building a master schedule these days starts with the selection of the project management software that will be used to schedule and manage the project. If you are using a skilled project manager, odds are she already has experience in such project management packages. You may also be able to count on your organization's Information Technology department to provide you with the needed software package and maybe even somebody to run it for you.

As a word of warning, our experience has been that many organizations elect to use project management software that is much more powerful (and therefore much more complex) than needed. Microsoft Project has more than enough functionality for even a major organizational change.

The high-level master schedule can be developed around the change sequence shown earlier in this chapter. The detailed master schedule can be completed after the change leader has a feel for the needed alterations. Input for developing the master schedule can come directly from the lists of needed alterations discussed during the previous chapters on alterations.

1. The vision (the detailed version as described in Chapter Two)
2. Work process alterations (as described in Chapter Three)
3. FET alterations (as described in Chapter Four)
4. Performance system alterations (as described in Chapter Five)

While a project management assistant might be able to make the first pass at getting these lists of needed alterations into the project management software, it is the responsibility of the project manager to sit down with that list of activities and turn it into a schedule. We have found this task to work better if the project manager and her assistant also have the time and energy of some of the people who produced the lists of project alterations. Their input will be invaluable in identifying the three critical parameters needed for a critical path schedule: the sequence of alteration steps, the estimated time to make those alterations, and the staffing required to make the alterations.

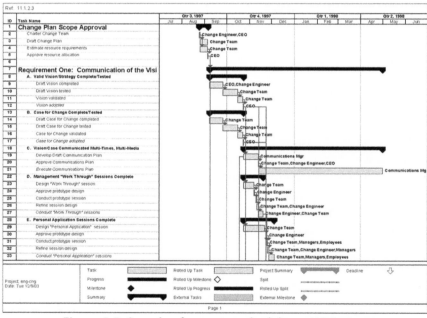

Figure 5.5: Sample of a master schedule on MS Project

Theory aside, organization members need to see answers to questions like, "What do we do on Monday morning? Is the work process training scheduled for this week or next week? And is that T1 (system) or T2 (work process) training? When is the new FET going to be available on workers' desk tops, and so on. That's where the master schedule comes in, showing the overall flow of implementation

ROBERT CUYLER, PHD AND DUTCH HOLLAND, PHD

tasks that must be done as well as the particular tasks to be completed by workers at each level and in each department.

Odds are that multiple rounds of scheduling might need to occur before the change leader settles on the master schedule she wants to communicate. For example, one round of scheduling might be made using the desired target date for change-over to the new work. This will need to be done first if the change leader has named a desired timeframe during the development of the vision. This step frequently shows that "you can't get there from here" as the old saying goes ... meaning that all the needed change work may not be possible before the desired new work date.

The second round of scheduling might start with the current date to calculate the projected finish of the change effort. The outcome of this round gives direct feedback on the realism of the original desired change-over date. The change leader can re-work the scheduling process as needed, adjusting time estimates where possible to get a master schedule she can live with.

Communicating the master schedule

The change leader must communicate the master schedule to the key managers of the organization who must be cognizant of the change so that they are prepared to lead their department's share of the change work and to shift to the new work at the targeted change-over date. Since the master schedule will contain a lot of detail (given, of course, the magnitude of the change), all of the organization's managers don't need to see all of the schedule; they just need the parts that involve them and their units.

The only practical means for communicating the master schedule to the managers in an already-busy organization is with a face-to-face meeting with them. Until then, the master schedule is just another email attachment or floating piece of paper!

The change leader must also create the conditions under which the master schedule will be heard as official notification of actions that must be taken by the involved managers in the organization. If organization members see the master schedule as "for your information only" (FYI) or nice to know information, they clearly will not be positioned to contribute to an organizational change ... on target, on time, and on budget.

Developing the change budget

Organizations that have mastered change can not only bring in a change on target and on time but on budget. The logical exercise that goes on along with the master scheduling process is project costing. Experienced change leaders know that changing an organization takes real money out of pocket just like building a house takes money. The elements of an organizational change that cost the most money are frequently associated with alterations or acquisitions of new FET. However, other alterations also take money. Listed below are some of those parts of a major organizational change that generate costs for the project budget.

- Development of the vision, frequently requiring professional fees for consultants, market research, benchmarking, etc.

- Alteration of work processes and writing procedures requiring overtime or professional services fees

- Alteration of FET including costs of Engineering and Construction vendors and the disposition costs of old FET

- Alteration of worker roles including training costs, new uniforms, possible salary adjustments, etc.

- Addition of extra personnel to work the change including contract programmers for software applications development/modification, Project Management and/or Change Management specialists to support the work of the change leader and the organization's managers

The idea is to get to a sound estimate of the cost of organizational change by estimating the costs of the pieces of organizational change. We have used two different approaches that work reasonably well for getting at the costs of organizational change. The first approach might be called the Proposal Approach. In this approach, the change leaders ask that specific effort and cost proposals be prepared for each identified part of the organizational change as it is planned. Over time an organization can build up a history of change project costs that will be useful for such proposals.

The second approach might be called the business plan approach that calls

ROBERT CUYLER, PHD AND DUTCH HOLLAND, PHD

for the change leader to look at the organizational change as the start-up of a new business. Business people who have approached a bank about a loan for a new business quickly find out that they need a pretty thorough business plan to convince the banker that their dollars will be well invested. A convincing business plan shows the structure of the desired new business, the vision, and the revenues that can be expected. In addition the plan must show all the important moving parts that will ensure the vision is reached.

The business plan will need to identify all the actions and assets needed to reach the vision and the total costs that will be required. We have asked numerous clients to prepare a business plan for change as a part of change management. Results have varied from consistently good business plans from some companies to mediocre plans at best from others. One clear positive result for requiring the business plan, however, is that the requirement forces the changing organization into a mindset that explicitly recognizes the financial costs of change.

Beyond these two approaches, we do have one last resort method to use in the absence of any organized change budgeting. We usually recommend the simple rule of thumb: determine the costs of the new or altered FET and at least double that figure to get an order of magnitude of the total costs that will be incurred in the change project.

Few companies today will launch a major capital expenditure project without a time schedule or cost budget … but it is quite common for organizations to undertake a major organizational change with neither, except for those parts of the change that involve a construction project for some of the visible FET. Organizations that want to master change must treat scheduling and budgeting for change just as seriously as they treat budgets and schedules for the normal work of the organization such as making and selling products/services or treating patients.

Northwest Memorial Example: Set and Communicate the Master Schedule for Change Work

The System Specialty Integration (SSI) master schedule was personally managed by the Chief Strategy Officer and the Telemedicine Coordinator. The schedule was communicated by sending copies of upcoming activities to the administrators of each department whose job it was to keep department members informed. As you would expect, some administrators handled the communication better than others and some department members were more likely to follow the schedule than others.

The overall status of progress on the master schedule was covered by the Chief Strategy Officer in the weekly meeting with the Executive Committee, whose membership included the Chief Medical Officer. Senior managers could hear their departments reported on schedule or they could take their eyes off the ball and see the Chief Medical Officer's expression when he heard 'off schedule'.

DID YOU NOTICE

1. The change leader must personally manage the project schedule (or have a close associate do it while sitting side by side with the change leader).
2. Get the laggards who will not follow the schedule under control by:
   a. Reminding them of their commitment to the change, or, if that does not work,
   b. Embarrass them publically in implementation status meetings.

Medi-Tel Example: Set and Communicate the Master Schedule for Change Work

Dr. Jannsen had been accustomed to working ad hoc with nothing more than a general schedule in his head prior to launching Medi-Tel. Upon being exposed to concepts of Change Management by Mr. Ames, his perspective changed completely and he was eager to identify the actions needed to put Medi-Tel on the map and then to get those needed actions onto a master schedule that covered the next two years.

Items on the Medi-Tel master schedule included a detailed communications program, a public relations program, a business development tracking system for following up leads, training for new

ROBERT CUYLER, PHD AND DUTCH HOLLAND, PHD

customers, a timeline for adding and training contract physicians, and a multitude of other small business fundamentals. Once the change schedule was down in 'black and white,' Dr. Janssen and Mr. Ames ruthlessly managed to the schedule, not putting up with obstacles or resistance.

DID YOU NOTICE

1. Did you just read that? "... ruthlessly managed to the schedule, not putting up with obstacles or resistance." Walk loudly and carry a big stick!
2. If you are managing the implementation of a telemedicine practice, you may need to walk softly and wear a big grin.
3. Along with the grin, be consistent, persistent, and firm, and you will be surprised how much influence you can have over the implementation.

Requirement 5C: Use week-at-a-time scheduling with one-on-one assignments

> *Mind-Clearing Example – Imagine a Director who is transitioning her theater company while continuing to perform the old play. Imagine the Director continuing to use a detailed daily schedule of performances for the old play (specific days and times for each performance, days when there will be cast substitutions, etc.). At the same time the director uses only a high-level schedule for transition to the new play showing only what months will be devoted to casting, costume fittings, rehearsals, etc.*

This step is a simple but often-neglected one. While managers in the organization that is changing need a master schedule to understand what they must do and when they must do it, their workers don't need a detailed schedule of the entire project. The workers do need an overall time frame for making the organizational change. But what they need more is a time schedule that fits their normal work routines. If the current work of their organization is scheduled on a once-a-week basis, change work schedules (for training, new equipment testing, etc.) need to be served up on a once-a-week schedule as well.

If we want workers to continue to do their assigned work in producing products and services while doing change work, we must help them by providing both lead times and scheduling of change work (like training, writing procedures, breaking in new equipment, etc.) that allows them to make the inevitable adjustments that must be made during times of change. Failure to keep workers informed of change activities has been the downfall of many changing organizations. There are few things that hurt worker morale more than having them surprised by elements of the organizational change that impact them directly. The kinds of surprises that we have seen while doing our change management consulting range from the simple, hardly consequential surprise, to what appear to be life-changing surprises:

- Surprise re-locations of the department, including worker desks and on-the-spot moves to another plant – today!
- Disconnecting of phone and/or computer lines without warning to workers
- Changes in signage renaming departments or work processes
- Impromptu training classes that workers did not know they were to attend or had no time to attend, given their other work responsibilities
- Unexpected arrival of new equipment or tools, or departure of old equipment and tools

The goal should be to have each worker see the change work that will be needed from him in time for him to get it done ... along with the old work that he is still doing on a day-to-day basis. For each week/month of the implementation, we want to show those communication and alteration tasks to be accomplished that week. Keeping well planned and followed schedules for change work in front of workers on a week-to-week or month-to-month basis not only keeps workers informed, but it pays extra benefits as well:

- It says to workers that change work is a regular part of our business along with old work
- It says to workers that the organization cares enough about them to keep them informed about what is happening in the place where they work
- It shows orderly progress toward a targeted change-over to new work letting the workers know that the organization is really serious about change.

ROBERT CUYLER, PHD AND DUTCH HOLLAND, PHD

> *Mind-Clearing Example – Imagine a Director who schedules all of the actors in his company to show up for a costume fitting at the same time ... when the seamstress can only handle the one-hour fittings of one actor at a time.*
>
> *Imagine the Director saying, "Well, I can't do everything for you ... surely you can handle a little scheduling problem!"*

So, where are we? We have developed a vision (i.e., an up-and-running telemedicine practice) and communicated that vision across the organization, with particular emphasis on the parts of the organization that will be most affected. We have identified all the alterations that will need to be made in the organization's work processes and FET. We have identified the individuals who will be impacted by the change, and we have determined the role alterations that will need to be made by those folks to be in sync with the new telemedicine work. We have already had an important one-on-one conversation with each affected employee to get him or her under agreement to perform the needed telemedicine work after change-over, to continue old work until change-over, and to perform the needed change work to get ready for change-over.

This step is designed to ensure that each worker involved in an organizational change knows exactly what change work she needs to do literally every day until change over. We recommend that managers use one-on-one meetings with each employee affected by an impending change to officially launch the change work that will need to be done by the employee. This one-on-one meeting reaffirms that we have the worker under agreement to do the change work.

We have found that change work gets kicked off much better with much greater likelihood of results when there has been a face-to-face conversation between manager and employee about upcoming events such as training classes, office moves, familiarization sessions on new equipment, etc. Merely posting a change schedule on a bulletin board near affected workers will not get them launched on the path to change.

After the one-on-one conversation about change work, workers may continue to address change work as needed with the assistance of a weekly schedule.

But more one-on-one conversations will need to be held during scheduled change work to ensure that the worker has the support, direction, and resources necessary to get the change work done along with his old work.

We must keep the workers' situation in clear perspective to ensure that we can support this critical step in organizational change. It is critical to keep in mind that workers in the midst of change are like the theater company members who are called on to perform the old play every evening while they spend parts of the day-time hours getting ready for the new play. During this critical phase of completing change work, workers still have responsibility for completing old work during the time periods when they will also be attending training classes, executing office moves, and so on. It falls to the manager of those workers to provide the support needed to be able to accomplish two critical things at once. Managers can arrange to have other workers cover for those workers who are in training classes, arrange for temporary employees to do some of the old work – or the change work for that matter (such as executing parts of office moves).

This one-on-one meeting step calls for some big shifts in what many managers do on a daily basis. It is quite common for managers in a smoothly running organization doing old work to have very infrequent contact with workers. After all, everybody knows what to do and how to do it and everybody is going about business as usual. When it is time for change work to get done in an orderly and systematic way, it is critical that the manager change the frequency of contact with workers. Bottom line, we want to ensure that each individual who has a task to do in implementation of a change has a clear assignment and responsibility for doing that work and has the day-by-day support of her supervisor in getting that work done.

Norwest Memorial Example: Use week-at-a-time scheduling with one-on-one assignments

Weekly meetings held by the Telemedicine Coordinator also allowed communicating of assignments, coordinating task force meetings, announcing training schedules, etc. There were so many moving parts to organizing the roll-out among the three specialties and four hospitals that implementation assignments were put on line on a shared Outlook calendar and task lists that had been constructed just for communication during the implementation phase.

ROBERT CUYLER, PHD AND DUTCH HOLLAND, PHD

1. Get organized about giving workers the schedules they need to get their change work done.
2. Without someone who loves counting widgets, the change leader can easily become lost and unable to manage the implementation.

Requirement 5D: Regularly measure transition progress and re-schedule as needed

> *Mind-Clearing Example – Imagine a Director who sets a schedule for the transition period to the new play but who never checks the schedule. When asked by the Producer how the transition is going, the Director says, "Oh I gave you and the company a schedule a couple of months ago when we started the transition."*

"Never a horse that ain't been rode, never a cowboy that ain't been thrown." And never a change effort that goes just the way it is planned. Change leaders can count on many things about the organizational change to go differently than planned. This fact does not in any way lessen the need for good planning and scheduling. They are the best tools for dealing with the inevitable interruptions, diversions, and obstacles that appear almost by magic in the path of every organizational change. Organizations that have mastered change expect the unexpected, and continually monitor for implications for the change initiative, aggressively re-scheduling change work to keep the overall change initiative on track, and clearly and quickly re-communicating modified schedules.

Expect the unexpected

The change leader can count on several of the following situations to occur on his watch:

*   Shifts in demand for the organization's goods and services
*   Turnover of key members of the organization
*   Problems with key customers or referring physicians (they change a big order, they cancel a big order, they stop making referrals, and so on)

- Competitive challenges (introduction of competitive products, decreases in competitor prices)
- Interruption of critical supplies to the organization
- Introduction of new regulations or organizational policies.

In addition to the situations above, the change leader can expect there to be surprises in the change work itself:

- Equipment installation takes longer and costs more than planned
- Equipment that gets installed but doesn't work the way it was intended
- Training sessions that do not enable employees to achieve the needed level of proficiency
- Workers who change their minds about staying in their current position and moving to the new way of doing business
- Communication glitches that foster confusion and misunderstanding
- Change leaders such as key task force members, project schedulers, etc. who leave the organization or transfer to a part of the organization that is not involved in the change, and so on.

When these inevitable situations occur, the change leader must face two realities: first, these situations must be satisfactorily handled, and, second, the organizational change initiative must continue movement toward the change … on target, on time, and on budget. There are, of course, some situations that occur that might cause the change initiative to be cancelled, but those are usually rare. Now is the time for the project manager to hold the fort and show the flag.

Monitor for implications for change work

Imagine a director who was so engrossed in preparation for his company's new play that he did not notice major problems in the night-to-night performance of the old play. Closer to reality for most of us, image the change leader who is so intent on making the organizational change on target, on time, and on budget that she does not see what is happening to the current work of the organization. The change leader must be focused both on the running of today's business (because that's what pays the current bills for the organization!) and the changing of the organization (because that's what will pay the bills in the future!).

As each day goes by, the change leader must identify those situations which might impact his change effort and determine the potential implications of those

ROBERT CUYLER, PHD AND DUTCH HOLLAND, PHD

situations. The two major kinds of implications that we want to watch for are as follows:

- **Obstacles to change work:** Situations will arise that could require an organizational response that will in some way interrupt the important actions on the master schedule and/or the change budget. An example might be a crisis eruption with an important customer that requires most of the personnel in a department to drop everything and rescue the situation even though they were scheduled for training on new work processes.

- **Issues with the design of the change:** Issues here are of two kinds. First, as the change begins to unfold, flaws may be found in the design of the vision itself. It may be that the potential value of the vision may not prove to be as great as once envisioned. In that case, the vision may need to be altered, requiring modifications in the change work to be done. Second, the business environment outside the organization might change, impacting the potential effectiveness of the vision. Once again, the vision may require modification.

Re-schedule to keep momentum

The two main drivers to the re-scheduling process are (1) the interruptions and obstacles that we have just discussed and (2) what the organization is learning during the change process. As the change work unfolds in the organization, some parts of the change are likely to go better than expected. For example, we could learn that training a department in the new work processes takes only half as long as expected. Or we might learn that the installation of FET costs less and/or occurred faster than originally planned. Any of the things learned during the change might be used to produce a re-schedule that is more effective and/or more efficient. Managers who have mastered change expect to see these learnings and are prepared to take advantage of them quickly in the re-schedule and re-budget process.

There are two approaches to the re-schedule process that we have learned to use simultaneously.

- **Schedule extension approach:** The first approach is to treat all schedule changes as alterations to the last and most current schedule. In this first approach, we are keeping the logic and sequence of the very first scheduling process in play as we identify needed schedule alterations called for by interruptions and obstacles.

- **Zero-based scheduling approach:** The second approach is like the familiar zero-based budgeting concept and calls for us to periodically re-think the overall logic and rationale of the entire master schedule. We stimulate this kind of thinking with questions like the following: If we were setting our master schedule today for the first time, what general order and logic would we use? Given what we know today about the organizational situation, how would we lay out the change work needed before change over?

The use of both these approaches produces the best overall way to look at re-scheduling. The most difficult change management environment our firm has ever worked in required re-thinking the change work schedule every Monday morning to take into account unfolding events of the previous week. Not every change situation will be as complex as this engagement, but regularly re-thinking the schedule has proven to be a critical skill for our consultants.

Yes, most re-scheduling efforts will be driven by the simple need to go around logistical obstacles. But sometimes we will find the clear need to alter the logic or sequence in the change schedule. The change leader must always keep in mind that he is doing two things at once: supporting the organization as it continues to do old work getting out its products and services to today's customers, while keeping change momentum in place for an organizational change that is on target, on time, and on budget.

Quickly re-communicate new schedules

When re-schedules are necessary, and they will be necessary, it is important to quickly and clearly communicate the new schedules to those organization members who need them. If you have assigned qualified project managers to assist in change leadership, they will be versed in requirements of critical path scheduling and re-scheduling. They will have established guidelines for keeping track of schedules to ensure that the organization always has the current schedule. Obviously in big complicated change projects with many moving parts, just keeping track of who has what schedule can become a big job. Clearly the current movement toward web-based project management and scheduling can be a major tool for ensuring both currency and availability of good schedules.

Unfortunately, strong project management will never be enough. Strong and diligent executive leadership must back the project managers and in some case, actually communicate any re-directs or re-schedules. Regardless of how well organized the change project, strong committed leadership with the right level of authority will be required every time.

Northwest Memorial Example:
Regularly check progress and reschedule

The mechanism for checking progress toward the build-out of SSI was put in place early, using the System Executive Committee's weekly meeting as the place to report progress and work issues. For the first few months of implementation, progress checking went along well. However, members of the Executive committee felt they were meeting too often and decided to meet only once every two weeks.

Unfortunately these meetings were frequently packed with daily run-the-business issues that squeezed the time for checking on implementation progress. If it had not been for the aggressive Chief Strategy Officer and Chief Medical Officer, monitoring of progress would have fallen to lower levels of management and lost much of its steam and sting.

DID YOU NOTICE ?

1. The single best place to report change progress is in the organization's regular "top executive meeting."
2. The primary change leaders in that meeting will be the CEO and the Project Manager.
3. Any deviation from the meeting and the leadership just described will dis-empower the change, and day-to-day operational issues will become higher priority than the change.

Medi-Tel Example:
Regularly check progress and reschedule

Having a dedicated project manager would have been nice for Medi-Tel but not needed in its first two years. Mr. Ames was so "into" the implementation of Medi-Tel he clearly was the project manager, the change leader, and the resource provider all rolled into one. His level of interest and enthusiasm were contagious as he checked on progress daily, gave positive feedback, and gave re-direction when needed. Imagine how other change initiatives might have gone if their leaders had performed this way. The business plan called for recruiting a new project manager in year two to implement new projects while Dr. Janssen and Mr. Ames ran the business. Mr. Ames worked hard to imbed his new business implementation into the culture of the organization so that a baton pass to a new project manager would be seamless.

DID YOU NOTICE

1. It is hard to beat an impassioned founder who drives the new venture from the project schedule in his head.
2. Change details can outnumber and overpower anyone, including a founder. The sooner a project manager is added the better.

Requirement 5E: Confirm, stabilize and celebrate the completed change

Mind-Clearing Example – Imagine a Director who hears by the grapevine that transition work has been done ... but who never goes or sends anyone to check to make sure. Imagine the director at a Pre-opening Night Party toasting to the company, "If it's not done by now, we'll find out after the curtain goes up tomorrow night!"

Old time managers who have "been there and done that" tell us to "expect what you inspect." Now I know that such trite phrases have lost much of their popularity in an era of participative management and flat organizations, but show me a theater Director who will move confidently to opening night without multiple dress rehearsals. Show me a Producer who feels confident to face investors with the words of the Director, "Aw, we don't need full dress rehearsals; it just wastes valuable time and puts wear and tear on the set and costumes!"

This confirmation step is designed to test the organization's final readiness to execute the change-over to new work. It is also about finding those last remaining trouble spots that must be ironed out before the organizational change can be made … on target, on time, and on budget. This step is one more opportunity to "Show the Flag" about the change that is about to happen for the company's betterment.

Make sure that alterations have really been made

The truth of the matter in change management is that the organization is not ready for change until it is ready, and a change over should not start without confirming that needed alterations in work processes, FET, and employee agreements have been completed. So the message here is simple: double check to make sure! But the change leader's goal in this confirmation step should be to come across as a leader, not just an inspector.

The best way to check and confirm that change work has been done is as follows:

- **Work processes:** Look at process diagrams for the new work; look for new procedures; see if you can find the old procedure manuals that are marked for destruction after change-over date

- **FET:** Look at newly-installed FET; view equipment tests; look for new operating guidelines; and view the plans for taking old equipment out of play after change over.

- **Performance management:** Interview employees; ask them to tell you about the new roles they will be performing; ask them to walk through the new work processes they will be performing; check training records; check their understanding of the change-over date.

Completion of these steps will provide some confirmations of change and some confirmations of problems. Once problems are identified, then the master schedule must be modified to reflect those actions that will be needed to complete change work.

Confirming readiness for change-over also includes checking for currency. For some of the mechanical properties of organizations, the saying "Once changed, always changed" just does not apply. For example, training records might reflect that training has been completed; but employees may not be "current." Training workers too far in advance of the change-over to new work will usually be wasted ... because none of us retains new knowledge or skill for long without putting it to use.

Celebrate successful completion of change work

So why do theater folks hold those "preview" performances, followed by cocktails for the theater company and selected members of the especially-invited audience? Preview performances accomplish a number of things that the change leader also needs to accomplish:

- **Final check on readiness:** Preview performances serve as additional dress rehearsals used to hone the theater company's readiness

- **Ending of change work:** Preview performances are confirmation with the cast that preparation is ending and the new play is about to start, symbolically moving to the performance stage

- **Thanks for change work:** Preview performances show appreciation for the hard work of preparation: "We recognize and value your hard work"

- **Commitment:** Preview performances are the last confirmation of full commitment of each and every member of the company to the new play.

Organizations cannot hold a preview performance as easily as a theater company ... but they can do something to get many of the effects of one. Preview performances can be held a department at a time or a machine at a time. Preview, preview, preview.

We recommend to our change management clients that they hold a celebration near the time of the change-over to symbolically confirm readiness and commitment. Such a celebration also says thank you to workers who have been getting ready for the change. We want the celebration to add energy, enthusiasm, and momentum to the individuals, teams, and units involved in the implementation of change.

Northwest Memorial Example: Confirm, stabilize And celebrate the completed transition

From less than a year from introduction of the telemedicine proposal, SSI had grown from an idea to a reality, with active consultations provided in each of the three specialty areas. The System was tracking improved market share in surgeries from the rural hospital service areas. Surgical patients enthusiastically embraced the option, which saved significant travel time and expense and improved cancellation and no-show rates for post-surgical check-ups.

Tele-cardiology doctors were gradually expanding the pool of patients for whom they would do initial consultations over videoconference, particularly if the required labs and imaging could be done by the referring rural physician and made available in the Electronic Medical Record. Response times for psychiatric consults were improved, and psychiatric length of stay in the system ED's was creeping downwards, but the program was no panacea for the limited inpatient psychiatric beds for indigent patients in the region.

The one-year anniversary of SSI was celebrated with a System-wide open house that linked via videoconference the board rooms of all the System hospitals, with attendance by administration, local board members, physicians, and other key stakeholders. The System CEO was lavish in his praise and gratitude to the many like-minds that had all pulled together for success. The project was widely regarded as a marker for much improved communication and collaboration among the System hospitals.

DID YOU NOTICE

1. Don't you love it when a plan comes together?
2. This ends on a happy note because Northwest committed the right leadership, using the right change methods to get right results!

Medi-Tel Example: Confirm, stabilize and celebrate the completed transition

Medi-Tel, despite many of the usual start-up glitches, found a significant market in delivering medical services to challenging and distant settings. Recommendations from early customers led to additional clients more rapidly than expected, with less reliance on traditional marketing than anticipated in the business plan. New business led to an expanded physician pool, lessening the call burden of the partner doctors.

The one year anniversary of Medi-Tel was celebrated with an open house that attracted other potential customers. A videoconference customer testimonial from an oil platform off the coast of Norway was a hit.

DID YOU NOTICE

1. Would that all changes worked out as well as this one.
2. This book's simple point is that changes can be managed to come in on target, on time and on budget.
3. Today, there is no excuse for failed change.

And in conclusion ...

Trying to lead an organizational change without project management will be an act of futility and frustration for all involved. The many moving parts of change must be managed in a very disciplined fashion or disorder will result. A major theme of this book has been to treat change work as a project ... using a formal project manager with the authority and resources needed to get change work done. When project management is used in conjunction with the change formula we have presented in this book, an organizational change can be delivered on target, on time, and on budget.

ROBERT CUYLER, PHD AND DUTCH HOLLAND, PHD

CHAPTER SEVEN

And in Conclusion ...

> *Mind-Clearing Example – Imagine a Director who has received the go-ahead from the producer and investors to transition to a new play. Imagine the Director calling everybody together ... actors, carpenters, costume assistants, lighting specialists, and the janitors ... and then telling them: "Hurray! We are funded for the new play that will open exactly 60 days from today. Let's all get busy!"*

AN ORGANIZATIONAL CHANGE is successful if it helps the organization move to a higher level of performance. We change organizations in order to make the future better for all stakeholders: customers, investors, and employees. Why go through all the effort of making an organizational change if it is not going to help the organization thrive?

Almost 70% of change initiatives fail to meet management expectations for two primary reasons: (1) trying to eat the elephant in a single bite rather than breaking a change initiative into manageable projects and (2) using what have proven to be invalid methodologies for organizational change. This book has converted both reasons for failure into right actions for successful organizational change.

1. **Right Action: Translating an organizational change into right-sized projects:** Successful organizational change depends upon breaking the change initiative into a set of change projects, each of which must be managed to completion. Failure to break an organizational change into tidy, manageable projects will leave an organization lost in the many moving parts and details of the change effort.

Figure 7.1: Multiple change projects for successful organizational change

2. **Right Action: Using a valid change formula:** Successful change project completion requires the use of a proven formula for making organizational changes ... on target, on time, and on budget. Failure to use the formula will result in project failures that may doom the entire change initiative.

Successful organizational change depends on use of the change formula ... communicating a new and exciting vision, creatively altering work processes, incorporating robust and powerful FET, and re-structuring challenging and engaging roles for employees. Successful change also depends on the use of disciplined project management that ensures that all the organization's moving parts are prepared and positioned properly for a new and better way of doing business.

Figure 7.2: The major parts of the change formula

ROBERT CUYLER, PHD AND DUTCH HOLLAND, PHD

The first requirement of organizational change is to construct a vision of the organization's desired future with a fully-operative and healthy telemedicine practice that will be valid, complete, feasible, resourceable, and engaging. Once detailed, the vision should be tested with members of the organization to ensure that it is an understandable picture of the desired future with telemedicine in it. To ensure that the organization is positioned to really hear and digest the vision, a case for change must be constructed that describes in some detail the potential advantages to the organization, patients, and employees of operating with a vital telemedicine practice.

Once the change vision and the case for change are complete, the next needed step is to communicate with all organization members multiple times using multiple media. This requirement is not complete until all appropriate management levels have worked through the telemedicine vision and case for change and translated them into action terms for their level and function, as well as for their individual professionals. The final step in this requirement is to test each healthcare professional's understanding of the translation of the vision for his or her job. Without this test, leaders of the change can hardly know if they are ready to move on to the next requirements of altering the mechanical components of the organization.

Failure to translate the vision and case for change would be like the director of a theater company who does not individualize the new play for each member of the cast and crew. Imagine trying to move to a new play without specific role assignments for each actor!

Just imagine how difficult it would be to give direction and keep track of a myriad of individual actions without project management lead by a skilled project manager. Also imagine a situation where even a good project manager cannot get access to and directions from the chief executive.

Yes, telemedicine continues to be an appealing and cost-effective option for serving patients in selected locations. All the technology is available, the dollars are available and appealing, telemedicine leaders are eager to show how this approach to treating patients can be effective. So what is the hold-up?

The potential of telemedicine is being severely limited by a lack of knowledge of the change management steps that must be used to get telemedicine up and running. Failure to master and use the change management steps in this book will forestall telemedicine success.

- Fail to use the needed change management steps and fail to produce a viable telemedicine practice or
- Use the steps along with a lot of hard work and commitment to see a healthy telemedicine practice alive and well in your organization.

The choice is yours.

Suggested Readings

1. History of Telemedicine, Rashid L. Bashshur, PhD and Gary W. Shannon, PhD. Mary Ann Liebert, Inc., 2009.

2. Telemedicine: Practicing in the Information Age, Steven F. Viegas, MD and Kim Dunn, MD, (Ed.), Lippincott-Raven, 1998.

3. Diffusion of Innovations, 5th Edition, Everett Rogers, Free Press 1995.

4. Why Employees Don't Do What They're Supposed to Do, and What to Do About It, Ferdinand Fournies, McGraw-Hill, 1999.

APPENDIX A

Task List for Successful Organizational Change

APPENDIX A

Task List for Successful Organizational Change

1. Transitioning with a clear, communicated vision

    a. Construct the detailed vision for organizational change
    b. Construct the partner to the vision: the case for change
    c. Ensure management understanding and expectations
    d. Communicate the vision the right way to the entire organization
    e. Ensure employee translation of the vision

2. Altering processes and procedures

    a. Identify process alterations needed for a transition
    b. Alter and test processes critical for a transition
    c. Alter process measures, goals, and objectives to match the direction of the transition
    d. Alter and test work procedures for altered processes
    e. Eliminate old measures, goals, objectives and procedures

3. Altering the facilities/equipment/tools (the FET)

    a. Identify the FET alterations needed for each transition
    b. Acquire/alter and test all the FET needed in each transition
    c. Alter and test each and every FET control
    d. Alter or create written guidelines for all involved FET
    e. Eliminate old FET and operating guidelines

4. Altering the performance management system

    a. Identify and alter individual roles and goals needed for transition

b.   Complete one-on-one contracting for every person affected by the transition
c.   Train all employees in the roles they will play after the transition
d.   Identify and alter the system for monitoring performance
e.   Alter and communicate compensation payoffs for work after the transition

5.   Project management for transition projects

a.   Set and communicate the master schedule for transition work
b.   Use week-at-a-time transition or implementation scheduling
c.   Make one-on-one transition assignments
d.   Regularly check transition progress and reschedule
e.   Confirm and celebrate the completed transition

ROBERT CUYLER, PHD AND DUTCH HOLLAND, PHD

Appendix of Detailed Steps and Scripts for Selected Chapters

APPENDIX OF DETAILED STEPS AND SCRIPTS FOR
CHAPTER TWO
COMMUNICATE THE VISION

A good way to get the vision detailed is to simply put a vision team in a room and ask them to write on wall charts answers to the following sets of questions:

- ***Organization Members:*** *Who will be working or behaving in new ways after the desired change is put into effect? How will they be acting that is different than they act today? What will be the accepted way they will be doing things around here? Where will they be located in the organization? Who will they be relating to or working with that is different than today? How will that interaction look? How will those workers be incentivized?*

- ***Work Processes:*** *What work processes or steps for getting work done will be different than the steps that are being used now? What parts of the organization will be doing things differently after the change?*

- ***FET:*** *What tools will people be using in work processes? What buildings in what location will they be in? What kind of desktop will they have? What software will the people be using in different parts of the organization? What will this software be doing for them? What will they be doing "on the screen" vs. "off the screen?"*

Once the vision team has sketched answers to the questions, the team (or an appointed small drafting committee) can combine the team's answers into a form that will make sense for the situation...either a short story format or a highly-detailed bullet point slide presentation.

Test the vision for organizational change

We think a good way to do the test of the vision is to get a cross-sectional group of a dozen employees together in a briefing room and ask them to answer the following questions (putting the folks into three teams of four helps the responses):

1. *What did you hear as the Vision for this organization's future?*

2. Can you see how this Vision will work to win with customers, investors, and employees?
3. What parts of the Vision need more detail for the sake of clarity?
4. Can you see the organization being successful in implementing this Vision?
5. Do you think the organization can get the resources it needs to achieve this Vision?
6. What about the Vision will be attractive, engaging, and challenging to the organization and its workers?
7. Is this a Vision that you could explain to others in the organization? What parts of the Vision would be tough to explain?

When you look at the responses to questions like these, you will know whether you have stated your Vision in a way the organization can understand. If answers from the test employees show that they understand the Vision, find it doable and compelling, you may have a vision that will serve you well in the change process. If not, clarify or add more detail to the vision. But whatever you do, don't start an organizational change initiative without a clear and understandable vision for the future.

Detail the case for organizational change

A good way to get the case for change detailed is to simply put the same vision team in a room and ask them to write on wall charts answers to the following sets of questions:

- **Customers and patients:** If our organization does not change its way of operating, will our customers and patients be more or less inclined to do business with us? How will our relationship look with customers and patients in x years? How will our way of working with customers be compared to the way our strongest competitors relate to their customers?

- **Investors and payers:** If our organization does not change its ways of operating and its financial results will our payers and investors be more or less inclined to keep their investment with us? How will they see us as a stock recommendation…buy, hold, sell, or sell quickly?

- **Organization members:** If our organization does not change, will our employees be more or less secure in our business? How stable will their employment be with our organization? What about development and training opportunities?

Once the vision team has sketched answers to the above questions, the team (or a small-appointed drafting committee) can combine the team's answers into a detailed presentation. This presentation must emphasize whatever facts are available to best make the case and to create a sense of urgency for the change.

Test the case for organizational change

We think a good way to do the test of the Case for Change is to get a cross-sectional group of a dozen employees together in a briefing room and ask them to answer the following questions (putting the folks into three teams of four helps the responses)

1. What did you hear as the Case for Change?
2. How plausible is that Case to you?
3. What do you see as the ramifications of not changing our organization's current way of doing business…for customers, investors, and employees?
4. Do you think it is important for the organization to change, given the potential ramifications to customers, investors, and employees?
5. Do you think it is important to begin that change now? Why or why not?
6. What do you see as the possible consequences to you and your job if the organization continues its current way of doing business?
7. What could happen to you and your job if the organization is not successful in changing the way it does business?

When you look at the responses to questions like these, you will know whether you have stated your case for change in a way the organization can incorporate.

Conducting management work-through sessions

Given these stated conditions, we have found the following structure to be useful in Work Though Sessions:

1. The organization's leader(s) start the meeting with an introduction that explains the purpose of the session.

   a. Our purpose today is to talk through an organizational change that we will be making to ensure the prosperity/survival of our company
   b. My expectation is that you will involve yourself in the session to fully understand the change that all of us, the company's management team, will be responsible for implementing.

2. The leader follows with a description of the impending change (e.g., the vision...including the organizational structure) and the rationale for the change.

3. The leader breaks the audience of managers into small teams of four to five to discuss and report on the following questions:

   a. What did you hear as the most important part of the vision?
   b. What did you hear as the most important business reason for the organizational change?
   c. What are the advantages to the company of the impending change?
   d. What are the disadvantages of remaining the way we are?
   e. What are the disadvantages of the impending change?
   f. What are the biggest obstacles to fully implement the change?
   g. What are your ideas about the best ways to go about the implementation of such a change?

4. The leader moves from team to team, making herself available for questions and clarifications as the teams work through the questions.

5. The leader calls for the teams to present their answers to the questions and arranges for those answers to be recorded for later use.

   • The leader's goal during this step is to hear the audience working through the understanding and assimilation of the information about the impending change.
   • The leader's challenge will be to hear these answers as part of a communication process and not direct criticism of the leader's choice of a direction for impending change.

6. The leader now shifts emphasis and asks each individual manager to consider the following questions for his/her organization:

   • What will be the ramifications of the change for your part of the organization?
   • In presenting the impending change to your organization (unit, department, section, etc.), what will be the most critical part of the case for change?

ROBERT CUYLER, PHD AND DUTCH HOLLAND, PHD

7. The leader might ask for volunteers (three or four managers) to share their answers with the audience.

8. The leader wraps up the discussion by asking the audience of managers to respond as one large team — because that is what they are — to the following questions:

    - On a one to seven scale, how clear are we on the vision of the impending change?
    - On a one to seven scale, how clear are we on the case for the change?

9. The leader records the number of responses in each category, one to seven (with seven meaning "very clear") and responds to the results. A normal audience that hears and understands an impending change will have a normal distribution of scores around the "five to six" points on the seven-point scale. If there are scores in the three to four range, the leader can ask the general audience (without identifying the managers whose scores were low) how she might further clarify the vision and case for organizational change.

10. The leader closes the Session with the following announcements:

    - We appreciate your input in developing clarity around the change statements
    - We will get back together again to discuss and finalize our action plans for implementing the impending change
    - Before that meeting, I (or your boss) will visit with each of you one-on-one to ensure we are in sync about the change.

Use proven communication principles

There are four principles that we believe are required for effective communication about impending organizational change.

1. **Two-way communication** — that allows organization members to ask questions and give feedback about the change — is required for a high comprehension level. We all need to interact in the communication process if we are to really get a message that is being communicated.

2. **Communication Bases** should be considered when planning and executing communication. In short, some adults understand new messages better if they

see them in black and white; other understand better if they hear them; others need to experience the message by handling physical models or imagining themselves in the described situation. Since organizations are made up of all three communication types, leaders must ensure that their communication plan provides devices that cover all three bases.

3. **Repetition** is required for any of us to get organization messages. While the number of needed repetitions has been quoted in the literature from three to four all the way to seven or more, our position is simple. Plan to communicate to every single person in the organization significantly more times than once to ensure the message about impending change is delivered.

4. **Rich, face-to-face communication** is required for organization members to communicate at maximum levels of effectiveness on critically-important subjects. Messages about impending organizational change must be delivered face-to-face or organization members will not have their communication needs at all met. Put the details in a follow-up letter that comes later…but put the essential messages about impending change in play in a face-to-face environment.

Face-to-face communication can be a real problem in today's world of companies that are dispersed over the country or the globe. Employees in dispersed locations have to hear about change in face-to-face meetings with their local bosses. And the local bosses need to hear it first from their boss back at headquarters. That usually means travel – there is no way around it.

Agree to and use communication standards

All managers involved in the communication of change must be in sync with how they are going to communicate to the organization. We have found it useful to get the mangers to agree on standards for communication that provides basic guidelines for the communication process.

1. Communication of the change will be done from a comprehensive, coordinated plan

2. All change messages will be developed and delivered ensuring that:

   a. There is a redundancy of message delivery (i.e., each employee receives the message multiple times)

ROBERT CUYLER, PHD AND DUTCH HOLLAND, PHD

b. The message will be delivered through a variety of channels (verbal, written, face-to-face meetings, newsletters, training programs)

3. All messages will be tested for understandability before delivery

4. We will ensure that our management actions match the words in our message

Imagine how well communication might work in an organization if all its managers agreed to and used such communication standards. One of the primary responsibilities of any manager is to communicate important messages about the running of the organization. When managers begin to take such responsibility seriously, organization change will get much easier than it is today in many organizations who treat communication as "just more of that soft stuff!"

We have found the following structure useful for the sessions between the managers and his team of employees.

1. The manager starts the meeting with an introduction that explains the purpose of the session.

   a. Our purpose today is to talk through an organizational change that we will be making to ensure the prosperity/survival of our company
   b. The goal of this session is to help you understand the impending change, what it will mean to you and your job, and to get your initial sign up for the change

2. The manager follows with a description of the impending change, (the VOC and the Case for the Change.

3. The manager breaks the audience of employees into small teams of three to four to discuss and report on the following questions:

   a. What did you hear as the most important part of the VOC?
   b. What did you hear as the most important business reason for the organizational change?
   c. What do you see as the changes we will need to make in our jobs in this department?
   d. What are your ideas about the best ways to implement such a change in your work area?

4. The manager walks among the groups making herself available for questions and clarifications as the teams work through the questions.

5. The manager calls for the teams to present their answers to the questions and arranges for those answers to be recorded for later use.

6. The manager now shifts emphasis and asks each individual to consider the following questions for his/her job:

   a. What will be the ramifications of the change for your job?
   b. What kinds of things will you need to change in your specific job?

7. The manager might ask for three or four volunteers to share their answers with the audience.

8. The manager wraps up the discussion by asking the employees to respond as one large team to the following questions:

   a. On a one to seven scale, how clear are we on the general direction of the impending change?
   b. On a one to seven scale, how clear are we on the Case for the Change?

9. The manager records the number of responses in each category, one to seven (with seven meaning "very clear") and responds to the results. A normal audience that hears and understands an impending change will have a normal distribution of scores around the four to six points on the seven-point scale. If there are scores in the two to three range, the leader can ask the general audience (without identifying the workers whose score were low) how she can further clarify the Vision and Case for Organizational Change.

10. The manager closes the Session with the following announcements:

    a. We will get back together again to discuss and finalize our Action Plans for Implementing the impending change
    b. Before that meeting, I will visit with each of you one-on-one to ensure we are in sync about the change.

ROBERT CUYLER, PHD AND DUTCH HOLLAND, PHD

APPENDIX OF DETAILED STEPS AND SCRIPTS FOR
CHAPTER THREE
ALTER WORK PROCESSES AND PROCEDURES

Use a Team to Identify the Alterations Needed in Work Processes

We have found that one of the easier ways to identify work process impacts is to convene a team of employees who know the organization very well and have them go through either the company work process inventory or the generic inventory and look for connections between those processes and the vision of change (VOC). The exercise that we use is a purely mechanical one. We give the team the following instructions:

1. *Spend fifteen minutes getting as clear as you can on the VOC*

2. *Working from the actual or generic inventory list, answer the following questions for each work process in your organization:*

   a. *Can we reach our VOC if the steps in this work process stay exactly like they are now?*

   b. *If "No," what steps must be altered to allow us to enact the VOC?*

   c. *For each step that needs to be altered, what should be the desired result of that alteration?*

3. *Compile the results of your team's deliberations into the following categories:*

   a. *Work processes that do not need alteration*

   b. *Work processes that do need alteration*

   c. *Steps in each work process that need alteration and needed result of that alteration*

4. *Label your team's compiled results as "Process Alterations Needed to Reach the VOC" and prepare to give team results during the Action Planning Requirement.*

Alter and Test Processes Critical to the Change

Use a Team to Map and Test Work Processes

We have found that a team of knowledgeable employees can map work processes to show needed alterations quite easily. After forming the Alteration Team, we give the following instructions:

1. *Review the previously compiled "Process Alterations Needed to Reach the VOC"*

2. *For each Process that has been identified as needing alteration, re-draw the process work steps from beginning to end, describing those steps as necessary to achieve the desired result*

3. *Mentally test each altered work process for effectiveness and efficiency (will this step work? Will it contribute to the desired result?)*

4. *Identify the kind of tools (plant, equipment, hand tools, machine tools, hardware, software) that would be needed by workers to perform the altered processes (more will be said about FET in Chapter Four)*

5. *Identify the staffing/training requirements for the altered work processes (number of workers, kind of workers, needed skills)*

6. *Identify the kind of real-life test that would be needed to insure the altered work processes will work*

7. *NOTE PROCESS AND FET EVALUATION WOULD BE PERFORMED AT THE SAME TIME*

After this working session, the most important thing the Alteration Team has to get done is to arrange and conduct the test of altered process. Of course the results of the test may lead to a confirmation or revision of the maps of the altered processes.

ROBERT CUYLER, PHD AND DUTCH HOLLAND, PHD

Alter Process Measures, Goals and
Objectives to Match the Direction of Change

Use a Team to Identify Needed Alterations in Measures, Goals, Objectives

We have used the same Work Process Alteration Teams to modify measures, goals, and objectives. We use the following instructions to get the Teams focused on the task at hand:

1. *Re-examine the "Process Alterations Needed to Reach the VOC" completed in an earlier step*

2. *Review those processes where step alterations are not needed, and answer the following questions:*

   a. *Will we be able to reach the desired VOC if all measures, goals, and objects remain unchanged?*
   b. *If "No," what changes must be made in measures, goals, or objectives for each work process and sub-process?*

3. *Review those processes where step alterations are needed and answer the following question:*

   a. *What measures, goals or objectives must be set for each altered work process or sub-process for the VOC to be realized?*

4. *Label your team's compiled results as "Process Performance Measures, Goals, Objectives Needed to Reach the VOC" and prepare to give team results in the Action Planning Phase that comes later.*

APPENDIX OF DETAILED STEPS AND SCRIPTS FOR
CHAPTER FOUR
ALTER FACILITIES, EQUIPMENT, AND FET (FET)

One of the easier ways to identify FET alterations is to convene a team made up of members of those professions who know how both the organization's current FET and new FET work and employees who will use the new FET and/or employees who will work in the physical location that will be the new FET's home. We give the team the following instructions:

1. *Study the Vision of Change, and understand what is being done and why.*

2. *Study the process, plans, and specifications that make up the new FET, and identify alterations needed in present FET*

3. *Find additional needed alterations in existing FET with a systems analysis of current FET. Conduct walk-through inspections of both the physical and cyber work areas that will receive the new FET. Identify direct connections that will need to be made between new and existing FET. Direct connections include physical changes, equipment, staff resources, training etc. In addition, look for changes in the indirect connections or impacts that may require alterations in existing FET or operation (upstream and downstream department impact, communication systems, supplies, etc.).*

4. *Discover additional alterations that were not visible on the walk through inspection.*

5. *Compile the results of the team's deliberations into the following categories:*

   a. *FET that does need alteration*
   b. *the kind and nature of alteration needed for each piece of FET*

6. *Label your team's compiled results as "FET Alterations Needed to Reach the Vision." Prepare to give team results during action planning.*

Approach Two: The process Inventory approach to Identify needed FET alterations

We have found that one of the easier ways to identify FET alterations is to convene a team that has three different perspectives: employees intimately involved in identifying needed work process alterations, technical folks who know the organization's current and new FET and employees who would be the likely users of the new or altered FET after transition to the new way of doing business. We give the team the following instructions:

1. *Study the Vision of Change and understand what is being done and why.*

2. *Study the alterations that will be made in the work processes in order to enact (the compiled report from the Process Alteration team is invaluable here).*

3. *Visualize the FET that would be needed to support the work processes that would be altered to enact the Vision of Change. Identify both FET that will need to be acquired and existing FET that would need to be altered.*

4. *Obtain copies of plans, processes, and specifications for the new FET and identify alterations needed in present FET.*

5. *Find additional needed alterations in existing FET by conducting a walk through inspection of the work area that will receive the new FET. Identify direct and indirect connections that will need to be made between new and existing FET.*

6. *Conduct a second walk through along work process lines. Follow the path of the organization's service from start to end of delivery, and identify the kind of FET that will be needed.*

7. *Study the plans, processes, and specifications for the existing FET that will need to be modified to discover additional alterations that were not visible on the walk through inspection:*

8. *Compile the results of your team's deliberations into the following categories:*

   a. *the kind and nature of alteration needed for each piece of FET*
   b. *FET that does not need alteration*

ROBERT CUYLER, PHD AND DUTCH HOLLAND, PHD

9. Label your team's compiled results as "FET Alterations Needed to Reach the Vision" and prepare to give team results during action planning.

A Very Special Case: The Alteration of Software

Regardless of the reason for the problem, the change leader must get in control of the requirement definition situation to ensure that the software alterations that are identified accurately reflect the FET changes needed to reach the Vision of Change. We have found the following steps to be useful for the change leader when she works with IT professionals in requirements definition:

1. Meet with the IT professional and explain the organizational change that is driving the need for software alteration

2. Go over in as much detail as you can the Vision of Change.

3. Go over in detail the work process alterations that are being made to accommodate the organizational change. Go over the entire work process change, not just the parts to be automated.

4. Work with the IT professionals to identify who will be interviewed and asked questions to identify user requirements for the software alteration (it clearly helps to have members of the Process Alteration team be a part of the population to be interviewed).

5. Have the IT professional walk through his requirements definition approach with you (this approach will largely consist of questions that he will use in his interviews with the users). Identify the questions in the approach that best address the FET alteration needs as you understand them.

6. Thank the IT professional for helping your change effort... then get out of his way while he does his work.

7. When the IT professional completes his requirements definition task, sit down with him and go over his results. Ensure as best you can that the requirements as defined will lead to software alterations that will support the transition to the organization's new way of working. And don't be surprised if what you find leads to additional interviews between you, the interviewees, and the IT professional.

Alter and Test FET Critical for the Change

Use Common Sense Management. For small or simple purchases or installations, it may be OK to use nothing more than the common sense approach…but it must be done in a very disciplined way…with goals, budgets, and schedules and so on.

Familiar common sense steps of management applied to FET acquisition:

1. *Get clear on what you are trying to do with the construction project*
2. *Clarify the construction budget and general time schedules if available*
3. *Decide on the equipment to be bought or altered*
4. *Contact vendors who sell or modify that equipment*
5. *Let vendors know what you want, and get a proposal/bid from them*
6. *Evaluate the proposals and choose the vendor(s)*
7. *Lay out the work of the vendor(s) on a time schedule*
8. *Calculate the total dollars likely to be involved*
9. *Secure management approval of the budget and schedule*
10. *Get vendors under contract and started on the job*
11. *Monitor vendor progress, and manage problems day to day to ensure the successful completion of the project on target, on time, and on budget*
12. *Close out the project with the equipment users, ensure their needs have been met, and ensure the contractors have been paid and have left the premises.*

Alteration of Software FET (i.e., "Clicks")

The bottom line for operating guidelines is equally simple but much harder to follow. Essentially we want to get operating guidelines that are no longer relevant, needed, or correct out of play in the organization. This simple task is made complex by the fact that many of the operating guidelines that are being used are not written down. It is always tough to get a written policy, procedure, or guideline out of play. It is especially difficult to get something <u>unwritten</u> out of play! But it can be done. The steps we recommend are as follows:

1. *Identify the FET operating guidelines that you want to eliminate*
2. *Create a written version of those "unwritten" guidelines (from what is already written along with information from folks who know the unwritten rules)*
3. *Get everybody a copy of the written version*
4. *Call their attention to the written version*
5. *Tell everybody that those operating guidelines will no longer be used*
6. *Take the copies away from them, and*
7. *Destroy the copies letting everybody see you do the destruction!*

ROBERT CUYLER, PHD AND DUTCH HOLLAND, PHD

APPENDIX OF DETAILED STEPS AND SCRIPTS FOR
CHAPTER FIVE
ALTER PERFORMANCE MANAGEMENT

ONE OF THE *easier ways to identify needed role and goal alterations and new roles and goals is to convene a team of employees who both know the organization very well and who know the details of the work process alterations that are needed. Have that team go through the two alteration lists (Work Process and FET) to look for contacts with organization members.*

We give the team the following instructions:

1. *Spend fifteen minutes getting as clear as you can on the Vision of Change*

2. *Study the Work Process Alteration List*

3. *Note any FET alterations that go with the alterations in work processes*

4. *Super-impose the firm's organization charts over the work processes that need to be altered and get a feel for which existing worker roles will be involved with altered processes.*

5. *Answer the following questions for each work process listed as needing alteration:*

    a. *Which employee roles touch the work processes to be altered?*
    b. *How will the roles of those employees who touch the work process need to be altered (i.e., how should their roles be modified to cause them to perform to the needed level in the work processes...using the needed FET?)*
    c. *What goals and objectives must be met by workers in the altered roles?*
    d. *What totally new roles will be needed in order to get all the work of the altered processes done?*
    e. *What obsolete roles need to be eliminated or portions of role realigned?*
    f. *What goals and objectives must be met by workers in the new roles?*
    g. *Which roles will need to work together as work teams to get the needed level of performance?*
    h. *What goals and objectives must be met by each needed work team?*

6. Next, as a check to the step you have just completed, go through the organization's existing organization charts/table and the list of all employees. For each position and for each person, answer the following question:

    Will this existing position/person be involved in the altered work processes or the altered FET?

    • If "Yes," add that name to the list of roles to be altered along with the nature of the needed role alteration
    • If "No," add that name to the list of Roles that will not need to be altered.

7. Compile the results of your team's deliberations and label it as "Role Alterations Needed to Reach the Vision of Change." Organize the list in the following categories:

    a. New roles and goals needed to perform work processes
    b. Existing roles and goals that need to be altered
    c. Direction of each role that needs to be altered
    d. Teams that will need to work together to perform the altered processes along with team goals
    e. Existing roles that will not need to be altered

8. For more complicated or comprehensive organizational changes, the structure of the organization chart might need to be altered to give the best structure to the individual teams and roles. Without going into great detail on organizational design, we want to identify the way we will organize units – individuals and teams -- around the work to perform efficiently to the Vision of Change.

9. Label your team's compiled results as "New Roles and Existing Role Alterations Needed to Reach the Vision of Change" and prepare to give team results during action planning.

Conduct the Contracting Session to Get Agreements in place

The contracting meeting is a business meeting, and it needs to have a planned business agenda. We recommend the following outline for the contracting session for an organizational change that will require major alteration in what the employee has been doing (for minor changes, the boss can pick and choose how much of the following outline to use):

ROBERT CUYLER, PHD AND DUTCH HOLLAND, PHD

1. *Statement of the purposes of the contracting meeting*

    a. *To get the employee on board for the upcoming organizational change*
    b. *To get closure on the role we want the employee to play in the future organization*

2. *Description of the organizational change the company has committed to make*

    a. *Explanation of the Vision of Change*
    b. *Explanation of the Case for Change (why make the change at all and why make it now)*
    c. *Explanation of how the work in the organization will need to be altered to reach the Vision*
    d. *Explanation of how the FET will need to change*
    e. *Explanation of roles that will need to change to support the work processes*

3. *Presentation of the offer to the employee*

    a. *Description of the role the boss would like the employee to play in the organization*
    b. *Description of the level/kinds of goals the employee would have*
    c. *Description of where the employee would fit in the organization*
    d. *Presentation of the salary/title change if any that would go with the altered role and goals*
    e. *Discussion of the offer with questions and answers*

4. *Ask for acceptance of the offer*

    a. *We want you to be a part of the organization after the change*
    b. *Would you be willing to accept our offer?*

5. *Clarification of next steps*

    a. *Effective date of the new organization/role*
    b. *Continuation of present job (Old Work) while organizational change is being prepared*
    c. *Participation in the Change Work needed to assist in preparing for the change*

6. *Meeting close with thanks for agreeing to be a part of the change in the organization*

CONTACT US

Our Locations

Change >> Force Healthcare delivers the flexibility of global reach with the responsiveness of local presence. We have offices near the Texas Medical Center in Houston and we serve clients across North America and worldwide.

Our Network/Alliances

Holland Healthcare Management extends its ability to meet clients' needs through a carefully selected alliance network whose members share our values, have a common service philosophy and compatible methodologies.

Call Us

Call us directly at 281.705.2775 ... our receptionist win ensure that your call will be answered as soon as possible. Email Dutch Holland at **dutch@ hollandmanagementcoaching.com**. Email Robert Cuyler at **cuyler@ sbcglobal.net**.

Holland Healthcare Management
2700 Post Oak Blvd, Suite 1400,
Houston, TX 77056
Tel: 281-657-3366

Lightning Source UK Ltd.
Milton Keynes UK
UKHW041245120619
344252UK00001B/429/P